Other works by Charles "A Castle Production"

Books

"Tai Chi for Everyone "ISBN 0-9545-7800-7
Order on line www.lulu.com

"The Journey Home" ISBN 1-4120-6602-6
Order on line Amazon .com "The Journey Home"
Order on line "The Journey Home" Trafford.com / 05-1513
Videos & DVD "Tai-Chi for Everyone" & "The Seven Set Practice",
E- mail Charles.

E- mail charlesjpshovlin@gmail.com
www.lulu.com
www.the-castle.8m.com
www.trafford.com
www.taichiworld.com

A WAY TO HEALING

THE SEVEN SET PRACTICE

CHARLES J. SHOVLIN

Order this book online at www.trafford.com
or email orders@trafford.com

Most Trafford titles are also available at major online book retailers.

Print information available on the last page.

ISBN: 978-1-4907-9822-6 (sc)
ISBN: 978-1-4907-9823-3 (hc)
ISBN: 978-1-4907-9824-0 (e)

Library of Congress Control Number: 2019918003

Trafford rev. 11/30/2019

www.trafford.com
North America & international
toll-free: 1 888 232 4444 (USA & Canada)
fax: 812 355 4082

Dedication

*I dedicate this book to all the light
workers in the new millennium.*

Contents

Foreword

By the Author

After practising my form of meditation i.e. The Seven Set Practice for a friend, she turned to me and said 'It certainly does not take you long to get there and you certainly have your passport back'. This so called passport has opened doors for me that I would never have dreamed of in the past. One of those dreams was opening 'The Castle' healing centre. What I really opened was my dormant family trait of healing others in need. That now means I see hundreds of clients on a regular basis in the hope of bringing them some peace of mind and bringing them back to their full spiritual awareness. The other great door that this passport has opened for me is the confidence to write, to teach people and to give them a better understanding of healing. It has also helped me to bring them to awareness that they too have hidden abilities and they should not be afraid to bring them to the surface. So this book is the results of many years of studying some of the martial arts, old eastern philosophies, various types of meditations including taiji, qi-gong and working with the earth's natural energies as a natural healer. Through these disciplines I somehow evolved to a higher level of thinking or inspiration or just perhaps my own imagination, call it what you like, but this has lead me on a journey to new discoveries which are talked about in the following pages.

Before these words were put down on paper I had a premonition of lecturing to a group of people. In these lectures I was teaching them about total spiritual awareness and giving them The Seven Set Practice meditation, to help them to open their minds to the great spiritual powers of the universe. After the premonition was over, I started to practice when everything was fresh in my head. The more I practised the more I became aware of my spiritual guide and of my purpose here on this planet, which is healing and teaching others to heal by these lectures and practices. At first I thought that this book was about my taiji and qi-gong training but as time went on the book took on a different direction. Even though I got strong messages to write this book and even what to call it, I still thought how in under God could I write a book on a subject, which to me was so complicated? At the time of the messages I had only been working as a practising healer for a few years myself, writing about it seemed incomprehensible to me. However, after all that had happened in the first few months of discovering my healing talents i.e. opening what was to be known later as the *CASTLE HEALING CENTRE* I felt once again inspired. I am thankful to have been able to listen and most of all to be able to react to such a request from the very depth of my being. Many of us get inspired in many ways but sadly not many listen and further more, many do not act on it. But those who have that inner knowledge and do act on it will not need me to tell them, that their life is full and rewarding. So *A WAY TO HEALING* was written by inspirational wisdom, to teach but not reform, to take away the myth of healing and to leave people with a clear open mind on the subject, so that they can draw their own conclusions. I hope you enjoy the read and good luck with the practice.

How This Book Came To Be?

These lectures were written in the space of two years and here's how it all began. After doing some meditation, I was relaxing and having a cup of tea about 7.30 am on the 25ᵗʰ of May 1996. There were snips of paper lying around from the sleeve of my video, "Tai Chi from the Castle". I was inspired to pick up the pen and start writing these messages down. I thought no more of it and began writing and during the writing a clear message inspired me to write a book and call it *A WAY TO HEALING*. This book was to be written for the benefit of all and one of its purposes was to take away the myth of healing and not to put healing into boxes where it is then labelled. As one knows if we label something it must stay within boundaries and this book tells us, that healing has no boundaries, only those we put on it ourselves.

As I started to write, the words could not go down fast enough on paper. This, I was told later by my spiritual guide, (in his time of 1500 BC), was what people call automatic writing. At the time I knew nothing about automatic writing and had little or no control over where or when it would happen. I would have to write regardless of who was around but mostly it would happen when I had quiet days between healings.

I would put the pen down but the messages would keep on coming, so I just kept on writing. Although it was relaxing and very rewarding, when I read over the material I wrote, I thought, I could not have written this and a voice in my head assured me that I did. I would find, after writing a lecture that I would be very tired, but even so, it would stay in my memory. The whole experience was very special and even the pen I wrote the lectures with was special as it was bought for me in a sacred place and given to me as a present.

One may ask the question here, how did I know that these writings were genuine. Well once I realised that these lectures were for the good of mankind, I knew they had to be genuine, as like attracts like.

I have already mentioned that after these writings I would feel very tired, more so than if I was doing a lot of healings. This, I was told by my spiritual guide, has something to do with the different channels and because these imprints or messages have to pass other dimensions and frequencies to reach the frequency my mind had ascended to.

I know now, after finishing this book that I probably wrote for too long. One hour is enough for automatic writing. I am sure many doors will open up for some of you readers out there after studying these lectures and doing the practice. Some will perhaps receive the gift of automatic writing though not all.

So a little word of advice, if what you are writing is not for the good of all mankind stop writing. On the other hand, if you think that these writings are genuine, be honest with yourself, keep your centre and go ahead and write them down.

Always ask your guide that it will happen at a certain time, so that you can get on with the rest of your life, leaving that channel or guide to carry on with their life in their dimension. Never write for more than one hour at a time, as this is very tiring and always be in control. Never ever become a slave to it or to any task or devotion in life.

Introduction

There are seven times seven dimensions, which relate to seven entities or energies of the planet. They are connected to the seven Chakras, sometimes known as the Seven Guardians of Faith and are also connected to the seven auras or magnetic fields around the body. They are all controlled by the laws of the Universe and are part of the whole governing energies. They are also related to the five seasons in Oriental terms, (the five seasons being Spring, Early Summer, Late Summer, Autumn and Winter). They are also connected the five Elements (wood, fire, earth, metal and water) and the 72,000 meridians or more that are in the meridian system of the human body.

To better understand this, lets start at the beginning and explain energy according to ancient cultures, philosophies and texts.

First you have the void or massive pull of energy and out of the massive pull of energy you have the two. For example, in the yin & yang symbol above, the tail represents movement and in the two movements of energy, you have the polar opposites of positive and negative charges; one side is yin and the other side is yang (Chinese theory).

So you have the two fish shapes (diagram). The black fish is yin and the white fish is yang and each one is carrying the seed of the other. The yin one has a white dot and the yang has a black dot.

This is what is known as the Eternal Evolution, each having its polar opposite as everything has its polar opposite. Yin flowing into yang and yang flowing into yin, day becomes night and night becomes day.

Now out of this Eternal Evolution, birth is given to all things - in other words the creation of the Universal energy system. So you have yin and yang, positive and negative charges of energy and the fusing of the two gives way to total balance.

In yin you have female, day and tai chi and in yang you have male, night and Wu-chi. Tai Chi is all movement and life and Wu-chi is all-dark and stillness translated meaning nothing. This is where we get and see the balance between plants and humans instead of the more obvious e.g. oxygen and carbon dioxide. When a plant is young it is hard and tough but when it gets old it becomes brittle and weak. When a human is young they are supple and soft but when a human gets old they become rigid and stiff.

☯ The Five Elements

Out of this balance of yin and yang, the "Five Elements" are formed which are wood, fire; earth, metal and water and out of these five earthly elements you have the cycles of destruction and the cycle of creation. The cycle of creation being that wood creates fire, fire creates earth, earth creates metal, metal creates water and water creates wood.

Likewise, the cycle of destruction is that water destroys fire, fire destroys metal, metal destroys wood, wood destroys earth and earth destroys water. So you have both cycles and these cycles are in everything that has life including the human body. These earth elements are stored in every organ of the body and in the meridian system.

☯ The Meridian System

There are 32 known meridians in the human body, of which 24 belong to the internal organs while the other eight govern other functions of the body. Each organ has a pair of meridians, one flow's on the right side and one flow's on the left side. One meridian is yin while the other is yang. An example of this is the heart, which is a yin organ with a yang meridian and the small intestine is a yang organ with a yin meridian. If you can imagine the meridians as a train route, then the pressure points represent the train station and the qi or chi energy represents the commuters. The chi energy is like the commuters who get on and off at different stations, as it too is activated at every pressure point. This is how acupuncture and acupressure works.

Let's look at the six main pairs of meridians in more detail, there balancing points, times and healing properties.

Balancing Heart and the Small Intestine Meridians.

The flow of energy in the meridians of the body, is from the lowest point to the highest point. We always start with balancing the heart and the small intestine meridians, because they activate all other pairs of meridians.

The Heart Meridians

The heart meridians belong to the element of fire and are yin property. They control heart disease, insomnia and inside arm problems. It has 9 pressure points; the balancing point for the heart is small intestine 11 and its balancing times are from

11am: 1pm These are the times where the energy is most active in the meridians.

The Small Intestine Meridians.

The small intestine meridians each have 19 pressure points; its balancing point is heart 5. They control eyes, ears, nose, fever, stiff neck and outside of the arm. It also belongs to the element of fire and is yang property, its balancing times are from 1 pm.: 3pm.

(This pair of meridians controls laughter and happiness.).

The Lungs Meridians

The lung meridians belong to the element of metal and are yin property it has 11 pressure points its balancing points is colon 11. Properly balanced; these meridians can help with problems of breathing, sore throat and sore arm. The lungs times are from 3 am :5 am

The Colon Meridians

The colon or large intestine meridian belongs also to the element of metal also, it has 20 pressure points, its balancing point is lung 9. It can help eyes, ears, nose, mouth, throat, flu and outside of the arm it is a yang property. It is a yang meridian going to a yin organ or bowel, it's times are from 5am :7 am.

(This pair of meridians controls grief, weeping and the ability to learn.)

The Triple Warmer Meridians.

Triple warmer meridian is yang property; it belongs to the element of fire and it has 23 pressure points; its balancing point is pericardium 6. Most people are aware of triple warmer 13 near the elbow known as the "funny bone". Proper exercise of these meridians can help problems of the eyes, nose, mouth, throat, fever, chest, lack of energy and outside arms. The triple warmer times are from 7pm: 9pm

The Pericardium Meridians.

The Pericardium meridians or (circulation / sex meridians) cover the internal fire in the body it also belongs to the element of fire and it is yin property. Each meridian has 9 pressure points and its balancing point is tripple warmer 10. Properly exercise of these points can cure heart trouble, loss of memory and inside arm problems. Pericardium 8 or (Laugung) point in the centre of the hand: is the body's energy point for receiving and discharging energies. The left hand is for receiving and the right hand is for discharging. The pericardium time is from 9pm: 11pm

(This pair of meridians controls internal fire, desires fantasise and the connection to all other pairs of meridians.)

The Stomach Meridians

The stomach meridians belong to the element of earth and are yang property.

Each meridian has 45 pressure points; and proper exercise of these meridians can help the stomach, intestine, eyes, nose, mouth, fever, deliriousness, chest and outside leg. Its balancing point is spleen 3 and the stomach time is from 7 am: 9 am.

The Spleen Meridians

The spleen meridians belong to the element of earth also and are yin property. It has 21 pressure points; and proper exercise of these meridians can help problems of the stomach, urination, sex organs and inside of the leg. Its balance point is stomach 36 and the spleen time is from 9 am :11am

(This pair of meridians controls worry, sleep and our relationship to the earth.)

The Liver Meridians

The liver meridians have 14 pressure points and they belong to the element of wood and are yin property, its balancing point is gall bladder 34. They control the function of sex organs, digestion, urination, chest and the inside of the leg. The liver time is between 1am :3 am;

The Gall Bladder Meridians

The gall bladder meridians have 44 pressure points; its balancing point is liver 3. It also belongs to the family of wood also; it controls the eyes, ears, nose, mouth, throat, chest, fever, out side of the leg and lower leg. It is yang property; it is a yang meridian going to a yin organ or bowel. The gall bladder time is from 11 pm: 1 am

(This pair of meridians controls anger, shouting and emotional disturbances)

The Kidney Meridians

The Kidney meridians belong to the element of water and are yin property and have 27 pressure points and its balancing point is bladder 40. It helps things like fever, control of fear, respectfulness, sex organs and urination, lungs, throat and inside the leg. A very important point here in all healing and in Chinese medicine is Kidney 1 (K1) known in Chinese medicine as the bubbling well point a point for bringing yin energy from the earth into the body, keeping it balance, grounded and stable. The kidney time is from 5 pm: 7 pm.

The Bladder Meridians

The bladder meridians belong to the element of water also and are yang property. It has 67 pressures points its balancing point is kidney 3.

The bladder meridians when properly exercise can help things like eyes, nose, mouth, throat, shoulder, neck, back, kidneys, hip, legs and bladder. The bladder time is from 3. pm:5.pm.

(This pair of meridians controls fear, anxiety and the ability to handle stress)

The meridians network is a wonderful healing method; and indeed it can be used as a stand-alone therapy and used along with acupuncture or acupressure. It is a very safe practice and does not require any great skills of training, all you need is good sensitivity for the body's energies and this will come with practice. However, before practicing it would be advisable to read up on the meridians and acupuncture points; to get the best results in balancing the opposite flows of energies in the body.

The Book of Changes

This theory of the ebb and flow of two opposite forces is all based on Chinese philosophy and theory and other ancient cultures, philosophies and texts. This ebb and flow of the universal mind has been the subject of philosophical enquiry since the dawn of time. But never has this philosophy of life been so well explained as it is in the Book of Changes, the I-ching written some 5,000 years ago (around 3,000 B. C.) by the legendary Chinese emperor Fu Hsi. All the great teachers and masters Fu Hsi, Jesus Christ, Mohammed etc. would I think be quite saddened if around today by mans separation from nature and the forces of the universe. This remarkable book shows us that man is not separate from the universe as yin is not separate from yang and that the flow of the universe is nothing other than the constant interaction of the forces of yin and yang.

What these old masters and teachers were teaching us in the past was true and indeed is true as we see now some 5,000 years on. With advances in 21st century medicine, science and physics we can now authenticate these teachings. We have the equipment and technology to be able to map out the body's energy and meridian systems. We can conduct these exercises under controlled laboratory conditions and different universities throughout the world have done this. We know the results we can achieve and it is no longer just wishful thinking but an actual science.

☯ Mind and Body Exercises

However, when someone says that it is all in the mind, that is true and what I am teaching in this book are basically mind exercises i.e. The Seven Set Practice. We are exercising the body as well but when we exercise the mind we can cultivate and enhance the body's natural ability and open up our awareness of the great spiritual powers of the universe that will put us in touch with our higher-self. This can only bring us far beyond any technology and science we know of today. However, we are not learning anything that we don't already subconsciously know, but we are relearning something we've consciously forgotten. The Seven Set Practice will help us to take control of our mind and mental thought and then we can create our own reality. This will lead us to a better quality of life, peace and relaxation and general good health (in perfect balance). So by studying and practising the postures in this book one is able to achieve their own potential in whatever field, be it music, art, poetry, healing etc. - there is no limit. The ultimate aim of everyone in existence is to be relaxed and happy in whatever way they perceive that to be. A person who is relaxed and happy makes others so. It is a natural thing that whatever the mind state of a person they like to cultivate that in others. So if a person is upset they seek to make others upset and if a person is happy they seek to make others happy. This all works on the principle that everything we do is a manifestation of our mind state. So by doing mind exercises you will gain contentment and good control over your health, free health, if you like. In other words, when something goes wrong you can fix it. Remember it's all in the mind and the thought is the deed.

Going back to science we should not forget and indeed we should thank modern science because without the knowledge of science these words would have little or no bearing or importance. The use of electricity whether it is coal, oil, solar, wind, hydro or nuclear generated, is only possible because we understand the concepts and laws by which it acts. Likewise, the use of the power of the mind is made possible through an understanding of the energy field that surrounds us.

☯ The Energy Field

It was estimated that in the 1950s there were only a handful of people in the world who understood Einstein's equation $E = MC2$ (the concept of matter and energy interchange). Now there are literally millions of people who not only understand it but also have advanced it. Throughout history there have been people like the alchemist or the wizard who understood the concepts of energy and they have held tremendous power over the people at large. Those who could practice energy healing or magnetic / vibrational healing were revered and honoured because of their esoteric knowledge. However, thanks to modern science this knowledge is no longer regarded as esoteric or hidden and is rapidly becoming common knowledge. Advances in technology have provided equipment, which allows us to see, and monitor the body's energy and meridian systems, which makes the concept of energy, interchange much more easily understood. Evidence of this can be seen in the number of people who are studying various types of meditation, taiji, qi-gong and vibrational healing. They are working with the electric or energy field of the body thereby causing the physical body to alter in the desired way. Homeopathy, Flower Essence Remedies, Acupuncture, Shiatsu, Kinesiology, Ki Massage, all types of Spiritual Healing Reiki and laying on of hands are just a few of what I prefer to call the complimentary therapies field. Orthodox medicine is also starting to use the concepts of energy more and more as in radiotherapy to treat some cancers and X rays, which are now an everyday occurrence in our hospitals. Weak electric and magnetic fields boost the body's healing abilities, in particular the healing of broken bones. This is an ongoing process and over time it will bring medicine and healing closer together. This is how I think it should be, as we advance positively into a wonderful and exciting new age.

CHAPTER 1
Qi-gong or Universal Energy

The Universal Energy System or Life Force system

Tai - Chi and Qi- Gong, (sometimes spelt Chi Gung) are household names in China, and are associated with a broad range of mental and physical exercises generally regarded as beneficial to health maintenance and health improvement. More than 10 million people there practise it.

Qi-Gong dates back to the Quing Dynasties of 960–1911 AD. It was used in connection with mysticism and many people shrugged it off as superstition, but with advances in modern science and physics over the past century, there was a resurgence of interest in it. Qi-Gong has been researched in the light of modern science and many of the exercises, which did result from superstition, have been tested and discarded but others have been retained. So in China today, Qi-Gong clinics have been set up to study and teach Qi-Gong and treat diseases.

Some common results of practising Qi- Gong are: gain in overall health; increase in energy and efficiency; decrease in sleep requirements while sleep quality increases; decrease in hunger and food intake; increased capacity to handle stress and be relaxed; increased ability to enjoy peace of mind and relationships with others; improved

1

self-confidence, self-esteem and overall quality of life. These benefits also apply to Tai-Chi or the old spelling Taiji, which is, if you like, all the Qi-Gong exercises strung together in meditation and therefore known as 'moving meditation'.

When we are able to break them down into separate qi-gongs and then string them all together it makes it easier for people to learn the taiji form and understand its principles in both combat and self-healing. Qi-gong postures done separately are most beneficial for those who cannot find the time or the teacher or the patience to learn taiji. I find that the best qi-gongs to do are the "Triple Warmer" and "Opening the Gates or Opening Quas". The four main gates in the body are CV1 (which is between the sexual organs and the anus), the lower tan-tien or (dantien) or navel, middle tan-tien or solar plexus and the upper tan-tien or third eye. These are the four main gates or Quas. The other Quas are between both arms and under the armpits and between the toes and fingers but these are not all that important in this part of the training.

Taiji is based on the energy system or acupuncture system, or the life force system of the body. The word qi-gong or sometime spelt Chi Kung, qi means energy and gong means work, so qi-gong basically means to work with the life force or energy system of the body. We do this all the time, the only difference being that in qi-gong or taiji practice we do it a bit better. We all need energy to walk and run but to run in a race we need to train. Likewise, in qi-gong and taiji practice we build up and harness this life force energy through breathing, just as wind harnesses electricity.

☯ Energy the source

Energy travels from a greater to a lesser source and in so doing must travel to the point of least resistance. It travels from the cosmic to the earth and we take it from the earth for our needs so we don't deplete our own energy system. If we are not drawing in enough energy, we will soon deplete our own energy system. This is especially true if you are involved in healing such as ki Massage, Acupuncture, and Shiatsu etc. If you are not grounded and connected to the source by keeping the Chakra system open, (see Chakras) you will soon deplete your own energy. You will only be able to see a few clients a day, but if you tap into the Universal energy you will be able to see many more clients a day, it will make no difference. You are not using up any of your own energy now; you are able to bring energy into the body through the Chakra system and your connection to the earth. When you tap into the Universal energy you are tapping into the source.

The Chakras

Eastern culture recognised the seven energy centres in the body referred to as the Chakras. The Chakras correspond directly to the seven endocrine glands of the body. These Chakras spin, stimulating the glands, which release hormones directly into the blood stream. These hormones regulate the function of all body processes. As we grow older, stress, negative thought patterns and pollution slow down the spinning of the Chakras creating hormonal imbalance, which causes the ageing process.

Taiji and qi-gong and The Seven Set Practice help to recharge the Chakras and return then to a healthy rate of spinning. They stimulate the lymphatic system and the circulation of oxygenated blood and balance the secretion of the endocrine gland so we have a quick and effective program to preserve youth and vitality

Each Chakra affects a certain part of the body and there is a different colour for each Chakra. The Chakras are explained in greater detail at the end of this book in The Seven Set Practice.

First Chakra

This is the base or root Chakra sometimes known as the "Fire in the Basement". It is situated at the base or bottom of the spine near the coccyx. Its colour is red, the colour of vitality, heat, passion and fire. It is the sexual or reproduction centre and is linked to the gonadal glands, sperm and ovaries.

☯ Second Chakra.

This one is situated at the pelvic bone and lower abdomen. It is the link to the adrenaline ie. the fight or flight syndrome. The colour associated with this Chakra is orange and it governs the kidneys and digestive process and effects personal powers, consciousness and mental energy.

☯ Third Chakra.

This Chakra is associated with the solar plexus and the left side of the brain and pancreas. It affects the liver and spleen. It covers our intellect and affects our self-control and it is yellow in colour.

☯ Fourth Chakra.

This is the Heart Chakra. It is our emotional centre and it reveals how we relate to people and how much heart we put into things. It affects love, grief, hate and compassion. A person may be light hearted, kind hearted or hard-hearted etc. It is linked to the thymus gland and the colour is green.

☯ Fifth Chakra.

This is the Throat Chakra and it is linked to the thyroid gland. It is associated with communication, both vocal and through gestures. It is beneficial for the neck and shoulders, where many people build up an enormous amount of tension. Its colour is light blue, which is the colour of energy, vitality and authority. Blue is also said to be the colour of healing.

☯ Sixth Chakra.

Known as the Third Eye or the brow Chakra it is situated in the centre of the forehead. Its colour is indigo and it is linked to the pineal gland. It affects the growth of the body, intuitive, non-verbal and inner vision and the creative right side of the brain.

☯ Seventh Chakra.

The last Chakra is at the top of the head and is known as the Crown Chakra. It is linked to the pituitary gland. It is violet or light purple in colour. This is our spiritual centre. It affects our involvement in art and beauty. This is the Chakra through which we receive divine wisdom.

Energy comes into the body through the Chakras. This energy must travel by some means. As the veins and arteries distribute blood, so too the meridians or the meridian system distributes this energy.

☯ Tai Chi and the acupuncture system

As any acupuncturists will tell us, there are 32 meridian pathways in the human body including two main ones that Chinese medicine tells us there are. The two main ones are the governing vessel, which runs up the back, the conceptual vessel, which runs down the front, all connecting to the (sushumna) or life force system. As we know there are over 72,000 meridians or energy paths in the human body, but we are concerned here with the three main ones especially the sushumna meridian or the life force meridian. To balance our energy system, we would use a relaxing meditation or mind state.

When we put our hands in a "hold the ball" position in the taiji form, this is only a physical way of getting the mind into a state of deep relaxation. It is the mind state, which is important; the rest is just an aerobic exercise. With nothing else in mind, taiji is just a good aerobic exercise. If we do not reach a relaxed mind state, then we haven't discovered how to channel the energy.

As far as the healing goes, without compassion healing will not take place and that goes for all kinds of healing from all walks of life, but this will be dealt with in greater detail later in the book.

The energy in the body will travel along the 72,000 meridians. There will be points on these energy pathways either to enhance the energy flow by pressing (acupressure) or to stop the flow of energy see (Dim Mak).

Taiji is based on the acupuncture system of the body. In taiji martial arts (Dim Mak) your aim is to cut off the flow of energy to the meridian and to the organ it is related to. Each meridian is related to a different organ - the lungs being related to the colon, the heart to the small intestine etc. with the lungs being the seat of power in the body. If you restrict a person's energy flow, that person will fall down. It doesn't matter how strong, or how fit, or how big they are, if you work on their energy system you can defeat them. In other words, if you throw water on the fire, the fire will dampen and if you throw enough water on the fire it will go out. It is as simple as that.

But in healing if you enhance the flow of energy or add more energy to a person's energy system you will release and open up blocked channels - sometimes this will result in pain.

An example of this is that if you close your fist and hold it tightly shut for some time, when you release it again it will be painful. The same is true of a blockage in the human body. A blockage that has been there for a long period of time, as in the case of a long illness, may result in pain while it is being healed or released. After one or more sessions in receiving healing energy from a healer there could be pain. This is why a client may experience more pain after a session than before a session. You must realise, sometimes things get worse before they can get better.

This is often the case with the weather ie. the calm before the storm. This is nature's way of dealing with things. But usually the blockage will release itself and the body will start to recover. The energy in the body will start to flow more smoothly and more naturally, it will also flow a lot faster. The seven Chakras will open up once again and return to a healthy rate of spinning. For example, when the throat Chakra has stopped spinning or eased off and is not as fast as the other ones, it is a sign that the person will be slow in speech or in gesture. So we have to open up these energy channels again by channelling energy to that person. They will, in turn, absorb this energy like a sponge absorbs water. However, they may be willing enough to absorb this energy but their destiny may not allow it or their higher-self may stand in its way. If it's not their path to be cured, then they will not get cured, as nothing happens by chance, as this is their path in life.

Most people are open to healing energy and are open to receive it. In these cases, mental barriers are removed to allow the flow of healing energy to pass freely from the healer to the client, so that person can be healed.

However, there's a big difference in healing and curing. Healing is where people get healed, physically, mentally and spiritually. If they get cured, well then that's a bonus. That is why people come for healing who are not sick at all. We all need our batteries recharged from time to time to lift the spirit in this fast changing, uncertain world we live in. I say, "is it the energy or the bulb that lights the room"?

☯ Realising your own potential

My aim in this book is to teach people to become healers and to teach them to stay healthy themselves. They can then heal themselves, heal others and also teach others how to heal and so eventually we may heal the earth.

However, this does not mean that after reading and studying these lectures in this book that everyone can expect to become healers. This does not mean that some people are better or worse than others as all people are equal and all gifts are special.

Through the use of The Seven Set Practice in this book, you may improve your own creative and natural abilities by unleashing positive energies and gifts that lie dormant. You may identify and break certain negative patterns, which may be preventing you from realising your own potential. This may then lead to other ways of healing, which might be more suitable ie singing, art, poetry etc. I personally think that singing is a wonderful gift and I believe that some singers are natural healers. Comedians too, are wonderfully gifted people and bring a lot of healing into people's lives, as laughter is the best medicine. We seem to have lost the ability to laugh at ourselves - what a pity? Working for the environment is another great gift, as these people are natural healers and sadly do not get the credit they deserve. What better way to teach people to heal than to look after this planet of ours?

That's the bottom line, that's what we are looking for. The objective is to heal this planet of ours, so we can provide a better place for the children of the future. To put an end to all the confusion that is going on in our planet in the 21st century. To open our awareness to the great spiritual powers of the universe, so we will have a better quality of open minded and open-hearted people around in the next century.

If, for instance, you wear a red jumper on a cold day, it will affect your own energy or aura and magnetic field around the body, as red is a positive colour with very strong vibrations. These vibrations will also affect the people around you. This is used quite a lot in colour therapy and in Chakra balancing, and because red is the colour of vitality and heat; it makes it a good colour to wear on cold dull days.

However, we must not wear all red as this could have a negative effect on our energy. It is the same as wearing all black or dark colours because too much of anything is harmful and dangerous. When there is no moderation there can be no balance and when there is no balance we know there is poor health.

☯ Mind State

We should all add a little colour to our lives as the saying goes "look on the bright side" and you will have an affect on yourself and others around you. While doing your taiji practice you will be in a nice calm and peaceful state of mind and it will reflect on everyone that's watching you. This is why it is wonderful to watch a true master at his/her art, no matter what art he/she has mastered.

We also can have the reverse effect on our energy and those around us. For instance, if you are walking around feeling depressed or agitated, it will affect people in the same way. Or if you have a drug addict or an alcoholic or troublesome person in the family it will affect the whole family, everyone is affected. If you have a sick person in the family everyone is affected. On the other hand, if you have calm and peace in the family or in the community everyone in the community is calm, peaceful and quiet. It's as simple as that. There is an old saying "you got out of the wrong side of the bed", and true enough it will affect everyone. If everyone so to speak is out of the wrong side of the bed, they will affect every single person that walks around with them.

If you wear bright cheerful colours, you will be a bright and cheerful person. It will not alone manifest on you, it will manifest on the person beside you. It is all a question of energy and vibrations, and energy as we know, travels from a greater source to a lesser source and follows the path of least resistance. It will travel from the cosmic to the earth in the same way that electricity travels from the power station to the bulb. The bulb does not light the room, nor does the person healing do any healing. A healer is only the channel for the energy to come through. So they are used as a channel for the energy to travel for healing or for combat.

The only difference in combat energy and healing energy is the mind state. Energy works on different frequency and variations and at different levels. If we give out something in a negative way, it will come back in a negative way and the same if you channel energy in a positive way it will come back in a positive way. There's no difference energy has no conscience whatsoever. It doesn't light the bulb because it wants too, but because it has too. You put a bulb up in its path it will light the bulb. On the other hand, if you stick your finger in the socket it will blow you away, energy has no conscience.

☯ Energy has no conscience

The switch on the wall acts as an on/off switch for the energy or electrics in your homes, schools, hospitals etc. The same applies to the body, with the on/off switch being the tongue on the roof of your mouth. By placing your tongue on the roof of the mouth it acts as a body energy switch to connect the two main meridians or the two main energy transmitting lines in the body we mentioned earlier, one flowing up the back and one flowing down the front. This produces a complete circuit for the energy to flow around the body. When you take your tongue up you make the connection and when you take you tongue down, you break the connection - it's as simple as that. It is the same in healing. The energy must flow around the body to allow us to heal others and ourselves; just the same as you would wear something baggy on a cold day as the air must circulate around the body to keep us warm. However, the energy will not heal someone because it wants too, but because it goes through that meridian to that organ on its path and in doing so it will heal that organ or give more energy to that part of the body, then so be it. For instance, as you are doing the "Brush Knee, Twist Step" in the taiji form you are opening up the meridian for the heart so the energy will pass through the heart meridian and must heal it on its way. In The Seven Set Practice, you can learn to manipulate the energy system of the body and attune yourself to the great spiritual powers of the universe. Not everyone can play music but everyone can hum a tune. We are not all Pavarotti, so healing to me is no more special than singing, as all gifts are wonderful and special.

Of course, if you have the natural abilities to do it, certainly you will be better than others, just as some singers are better than others. However, this will not mean that you will not be able to do it. Just like the singing, some will be naturally different than others and indeed some will get to the stage of playing music as well or even do the two together. Just as some healers can channel more energy than others. Some musicians will play different musical instruments than others but it is still music. In the same way some healers will have different gifts and powers of healing, but it is all healing and it all comes from the same source and everyone I believe can do it. But remember that before healing can take place you must have the energy, commitment and above all the compassion and then the rest is easy.

If, however, you try too hard or get too bogged down in what you are doing this will block the flow of energy and if for one moment you think that you are doing the healings then that too will block the flow of energy. There are no trophies for healing and you are doing nothing just being there. It is not your energy; you are a channel for the universal energy to pass through you and through the other person back to the earth to be purified. In so doing, this not alone stimulates the client's energy system but the healer's energy system as well and thus heals both as it passes.

☯ Healing comes from the Source

Universal Energy or Cosmic or Divine or God, these are just names. It is the same with names or labels for healing and healers. These are just man made names and titles to make that person feel more important than the rest. We all come from different walks of life but breathe the same air or chi. Names and titles are dangerous and cause confusion and therefore lead to an imbalance or disharmony between fellow men, nature and the universe.

Healing is healing and can only come from the source. The rest are just names or labels, as this energy does not belong to any one person or group of people. It belongs to the source or in our case, the earth. I think the greatest mistake of all cultures and religious groups or organisations in the past was, in believing that they had some kind of copyright on 'energy' and they made a big thing of it. Surely we must have the greatest respect for this energy but it most definitely does not belong to us. Nothing does, everything belongs to the earth. We must remember that here on earth there will always be greater and lesser people than ourselves. No matter where you go there are guides greater and lesser than you. They will still be your guides and as its the universal law that all things will be, and are equal for all, so we can heal the earth of its ways no matter how long this will take.

☯ Taiji and energy

This energy passes through points on your feet called "kidney one" (ki) which the Chinese call "the bubbling well point". When you lift your foot up off the earth, the energy comes up through "kidney one" (ki) and when you place your foot back down again you will channel the energy back down again to the earth. Energy will pass through points in the hands too in the same way, through "Laugung" or Pericardium 8. This point is the point of exchanging energy with the Universe, the environment and other persons. Pericardium 8 is in the centre of the hand; the left hand is for receiving the energy and the right hand is to discharge the energy. You can channel energy from the left hand to the right hand and the same with the feet, moving you feet from the left to the right, by making circular movement with the waist. This is explained in a scientific way as qi-gong is a healing science, but of course healing goes much deeper.

We do the qi-gong to help the healing process; there is no technique as such. It is just a way of putting your body into certain positions so you will stimulate the energy system in your body and help to heal yourself. Peace of mind and deep relaxation is achieved from the breathing techniques and energy manipulating positions, which you do during your taiji or qi-gong practice.

We do taiji in the morning for bones and muscles. In the afternoon for the mind and we do it in the evening for the spirit. Fast in the morning, slow in the afternoon and dead slow in the evening.

This is the same as our daily activity; all go in the morning, slowing down in the afternoon and getting very slow towards nightfall.

When we are learning taiji at first we do it very openly and very physically exaggerated so that we learn the correct pattern. Then by doing the pattern repetitively the mind learns to stay in a relaxed meditative state. At this stage, when doing one movement you are thinking of the next movement and you don't have time to think of anything else. You don't have time to think of the weather or who or what is around you. You are thinking of the next pattern that comes along, so it brings you into a state of meditation. In the next stage of taiji we will slow it down a little and do it slower than we normally do it. When we move slowly we train the mind to be slow, however, your reactions will be much quicker, as the mind is the greatest computer of all. This leaves it excellent for the martial art and of course healing. There is no difference; they work on different frequencies, levels and mind states.

☯ Taiji and the subconscious

The next part of the training in taiji is when we move in a subconscious state or move in a meditative state and are totally locked in our meditation. This is the hardest part of the taiji discipline, it is the easiest to do but the hardest to master. All the movements now become very tight and very small. Before this they were very open and very wide and exaggerated. In other words, now you close in tight in every movement. You cut out a lot of the big movements and you move in a circular fashion, as we know energy moves in circles and not in straight lines. This is most obvious if we look at the curves on the "cups" at the top of the electrical polls. The electricity or energy moves in a spiral circular fashion, right around these "cups" all the time. So at the last stage of our taiji practice we also move in spiral circular movements. The energy comes up the left leg via the knee joint, emanated up through the waist, up the back and down the arm and is discharged out through the hand either for martial or for healing purposes. It actually comes up through the centre of the body, (sushumna) but we relate it to the backbone, simply because we can see it and touch it.

☯ Three Back Positions

There are three positions for the back.

The first position is the "S" shape back. When we walk around every day our back is in an S shape. This is mainly because it is acting as a shock absorber so that we can bounce around. This "S" shape also helps to keep our spinal column and discs in shape.

The next position of the back is the Straight Back. When we bend our knees drop down a little as if we were sitting on a stool, this is a straight back position. The straight back is also apparent when you drop your knees and tuck your pelvis under or tuck your bum under making sure the back doesn't lean backwards or forward, just sit down as you are.

The next stage is known as a "C" back. All animals get into this position when they are in confrontation with one another as they are going to attack. Another part they will develop as well is the "reptilian brain" which is the animal instinct brain, which we have had since the start of evolution. Before we got a mammalian brain we had "reptilian brain" the animal instinct brain, this is where we just go forward not on the defensive but on the offensive.

By tapping into the "reptilian brain" the energy curves the backbone affecting the central nervous system to bring us to a subconscious state of mind and we take on a meditative or docile reptile look. This is not something to be encouraged as in this state we can draw ancestral negative vibration to us. However, if not practiced for too long, it has positive effects for the immune system, memory, peripheral vision or eagle vision as it's known in the martial arts world.

A reptile will not grab your arm and throw you over the fence. It will just sit there docile and when you come in on its energy field it will just bounce out and go forward for you. So many tourists have been caught off guard by these docile creatures, by getting too close to them.

So when the energy comes up the back it will change shape not because it wants too but because the energy is coming up through it and changing and altering the shape of it as it comes up. This is why channelled energy can put back discs etc. You are now at a subconscious level and the only time you come back into a conscious state again is about a fraction of a second before you strike.

☯ Taiji and healing

In healing, however, you stay in that subconscious state but your back will be rounded even though people may not be aware of it or may not notice it. However, the energy will be so strong coming through you and especially through your hands that it will feel like heat to most people or a tingling sensation. The sensation is usually experienced as heat or cold because this is how we relate to energy. When a lot of energy is created your fingers may get cold or numb and sometimes your hands may get numb as well. They may start to vibrate or shake and that is the highest form of the healing properties of taiji. Taiji will bring to the surface natural abilities in you that you did not think you could possibly have. In other words, it will bring out your own natural abilities, which you already have. It may stir up different gifts of one kind or another e.g. music, art, literature, psychic intuition etc. In taiji, which is moving meditation, you will develop your subconscious mind by opening up your brow or third eye Chakra. You will be inspired in many ways such as gaining very high intuition, intent, and insight from studying the taiji and doing the taiji & qi-gong practice.

So energy has no conscience whatsoever, there is neither good energy nor bad energy. It is just energy, and the use we put it to, by the power of our mind i.e. thoughts, words, deeds and actions - that's what's important. It is the mind that controls the chi or energy and the chi controls the physical. For instance, if we walk towards a door the chi goes there first!

☯ The mind controls the chi

It is the mind that controls the chi and the chi activates the muscles in our bodies. We need energy to activate any muscle in the body so once we get control of our mind we can control our chi, when the mind controls us it leads to great confusion. The mind plays tricks on people and causes confusion doubt and fear. You can conquer inner fear through exercises of the mind. The mind is so powerful and so tricky, you never hear anyone say its a sad day but we often hear the saying its a cold day and sayings to that effect. We could say it's a sad day or it's a happy day but this is just a state of mind so we have to try and control our mind rather than let it control us. So once we get control of the mind we will also have control of the chi energy.

Through the practice meditation taiji and qi-gong or the seven set practice in this book, we can channel chi energy to any part of the body and use it for anything we want. Some people will use it to do tricks or so called magic, like bending spoons and stopping watches etc. We can use it in this way as we all have free will but to me this is a great waste of universal energy, which could be used for a higher purpose. There is nothing wrong with bending spoons and stopping watches for a little fun, if that's what people want to do, but to make fun of others by doing mind games while manipulating their mind states, is to me a great waste of energy and can be dangerous.

☯ Connectivity with the earth's energy

This energy does not belong to us nor does it belong to any one culture, race or creed. It is not part of something we get, it is something that we have and that is channelled through us. It is not something that we want to control or let it control us but we must control how we use it, so that we can stay in harmony with it all the time.

Here, I will use another way of explaining the energy system and how it works. I am here, standing on the earth, which is stuck onto my feet, and also the earth is stuck onto the trees. What we are talking about here is connectivity with the earth passing energies, to and from us, all the time. This energy is being channelled from one person to another through the feet, which are connected to the earth. As we know our feet act as conductors drawing energy all the time to and from the earth. In this way we tap into the low earth ground frequency or wavelength. All positive or pure (in spiritual terms) energies are below the ground and all negative or impure energies are above the ground.

It may take a long time and many life times to be able to tap into the earth's frequency. Even if we could tap into this knowledge we would not be allowed use it in a negative way without destroying ourselves. Hitler is a good example of this. He overstepped his gift of free will, by controlling and harming others. So a word of warning, you cannot use or be allowed to use this energy to control or to harm others without destroying yourself, your higher-self (i.e. the soul). This is where the gift of free will is abused.

If you use your intentions (energy) in a good and positive way, it will come back to you 10 fold in a positive way. So through connectivity with the earth someone could be in another part of the world miles away from me, we may not have met but yet we are still connected. I have examples of this connectivity with friends all over the world. We never meet and yet subconsciously we are very close! So by the practice of meditation you are able to tap into your subconscious mind this is another channel to connect with people. So when two or more minds tap into one another or when you tap into the universal channel or collective conscious as it is sometimes called, then absent healing can be done

Absent healing can be done directly or indirectly (see absent healing). Directly is where you tap into like minds, as like attracts like. Indirectly is where we use a friend's mind to channel energy to that person. If your friend knows someone on the other side of the world you just link with that person's mind in meditation and use it to channel energy to their friend a far way off. It is as simple as that.

☯ Thoughts are energy

Energy as well as having no conscience has no limits. It can travel at the speed of light or the speed of thought and there is nothing more powerful or faster than thought. I am sure some day or sometime in the not so distant future we will have conquered time travel. I honestly think that this is possible in the way thought can travel, as thought is energy. A positive thought or a negative thought is energy or emotion i.e. energy in motion. If for instance you have a negative emotion trapped or blocked in your mind sometimes this may manifest itself on your body. We have a lot of these blockages around at present through the stressful world we live in. However, these blockages may be caused by a difficult childhood or a difficult birth in this life time or possible in another lifetime (see energy dimensions). This blocked energy will manifest on the physical body in many ways e.g. rash, extreme headaches, depression, pains and aches of one kind or another, to mention just a few. When a lot of energy gets trapped, it builds up a lot of pressure or emotion and sometimes this pressure goes to the head and so it gets trapped there, and this is not healthy. If the chi energy gets blocked there, the person may get severe headaches, depressed or drained of energy i.e. vitality. We must try to dampen the fire of trapped emotions through the water channels. This is achieved by grounding to the earth through the soles of your feet at kidney one (k1). By this practice we get the spirit to rise to the head and other Chakras and we get the chi energy to build up in the tan-tian an acupuncture point three inches below the navel. This is our body energy storehouse centre where energy is stored and circulated around the body through the action of *diaphragmatic* breathing or natural breathing. Energy should be filling up here in the tan-tien all the time like a kettle boiling over. When a person practices taiji and qi-gong, the chi will spill out over the whole body healing the body as it goes.

The chi will now turn to different states in different places. First it will turn to Jing qi and go right into the bone marrow and into the T cells, which acts on our immune system. It will then heat up and rise and turn to Shi qi. It travels through every organ in the body healing every cell in its path.

Next it will change to Zhen qi, as we know it in Zen (shen) meditation or spirit, and that is the highest level that you can achieve i.e. the level of enlightenment. The level of enlightenment is eternally present in the here and now. This very moment, the moment that went past, was not the past as we think of it but it was an eternal moment of the present here and now. It was an after thought of what happened now. The future will be an on coming thought of the here and now and you know you cannot live in the past nor can you live in the future, you have to live in the present, the here and now, the eternal moment.

☯ Bringing up the earth's energy

So eternal energy or eternal chi, call it what you like, comes in from the universe to the earth. It travels from a greater source to a lesser source. I remember chi energy used to confuse me as a young boy as I am sure it does most people. I used to wonder what it was like and what colour it was and what it looked like. Now 30 years on I know it has none of these things. It has no colour and is just what it is i.e. energy. Some people may see colour but that's how they perceive it. We conduct this energy from the earth by tapping our feet on the ground as they act as conductors. We can sense it moving through our hands and drawing it to us, as our hands are only used to help us to become more sensitive to the flow of energy We use our feet likewise, as some people can sense energy in their feet as the feet will get quite warm and turn a nice colour of pink or red in the practice of taiji or qi-gong. We can use our hands or our eyes to channel this energy. As in different qi-gong practices. Lastly we can use our mind or thought and there is nothing more powerful or faster than thought. This is the easiest of all to do, to channel energy, but it is the hardest to achieve, we need total mindfulness in order to achieve this.

Wild or cross animals will bring up the earth's energy very quickly, by stamping or dragging their feet on the ground and that sort of thing. They will bring up the energy but they have little or no control over it due to their reptilian brain. But the reason we have control when we bring up the energy is that we place our heel on the ground as we walk around. We place the heel of the foot on the ground first and the ball of the foot on the ground last as in the taiji or tai chi walking, sometimes known as ghost walking.

(Ghost walking was around before there was any electric light or street lighting. The villain would creep up on the unsuspecting victim, hide in their shadow and then easily kill their victim).

So the heel of the foot acts as a set up point or a balancing point for the ball of the foot Kidney one (K1). It will balance the earth energy and help us to have control over the amount of energy we channel from the earth. Wild animals don't do this because they have no heel and will bring up so much energy that they can't control it. There is no point in tapping into something that you cannot control. The same way you would not give a child the keys of your car as this would be foolish and could only lead to destruction

We must be able to bring up the energy and still have control of it. We do this by circling the foot on the ground in a toe and heel fashion. We can use clockwise or anti clockwise movements, it doesn't matter as long as they are done in circles as energy travels in circles and not in

18

straight lines. This is a good way to find calm and balance when giving a lecture, by moving your weight from foot to foot or from fullness to emptiness as in the taiji form. In this way you will make contact with the earth and bring up the energy without any one knowing what you are doing. When most people engage in public speaking they usually have a stand to lean on to calm the nerves, because their legs may start to shake. It is a chemical reaction or energy reaction in the body, cause by a rush of adrenaline, which can break his or her contact with earth for a short period. However, after some time of leaning on the stand, the mind will channel energy to the arms or hands. So now that person will forget about the legs and will start to relax and a different chemical or energy reaction will take place and he / she will get connected to the earth again. If for instance you are in conversation with someone or lecturing to a group of people and you think they are looking at you rather than, that you are an entity of energy looking at them. You are looking out at them but you do not see what is looking at them. You are a ball of energy (atoms & molecules). This theory will help you not to be afraid of walking up the floor and thinking that there is someone looking at you, you are in control. You are the one that's looking on and you are the one that's looking out. Now you will not be tapping your feet on the ground when you are giving a lecture. However, if you drop your waist slightly and move your feet back and forward shifting the weight of your body from foot to foot, you can talk all day with no problem what so ever. There will be no nerves or stutters and not so much thinking. If you start thinking too much of what you are going to do next in combat or any situation you will have lost time. You move on a subconscious level or an energy level and subconscious reaction. In the same way, as I am writing this lecture, the messages are coming in at collective level or collective channel. I have no notes in front of me the thoughts or messages are coming in through inspiration or inspirational guides. I am only cloaking them into words.

The main health property from taiji is relaxation and peace of mind. In meditation you achieve stillness of the body and stillness of the mind and above all stillness of the spirit. Where there is stillness there is peace and out of this peace comes power. This has got nothing to with strength or the ability to lift something; power is a presence of mind. So out of the stillness comes the power between the internal and external energies in the body and an opening or openness in the force of the universal energy system. Once you are very still and collected in your thoughts and collected in your ideas everything is under control you will be loaded with confidence. However, at the same time if you go to teach taiji or any subject of your choice it's important that you know what you are talking about.

In this way you will have the power to walk into any room and give a lecture to 50 people or 500 people, it won't make any difference, you are now standing in your own power. If you think of the number of people in front of you then you are lost. You don't think, you just go and give your talk as if there was just one person in the room listing to you.

☯ Dim Mak Pressure Points

Dim Mak pressure points or "Death Point Striking" as it is sometimes called, is a specialised technique requiring the striking of a particular point or group of points i.e. pressure points at a certain time of day or season to drain the energy from the body. It is either used to knock an opponent out or put the opponent into what is known as neurological shut down. This deadly art was developed by highly skilled practitioners through the centuries and is based on the vital pressure points and the various organs and chi, the emphasis is on the efficiency of the strike and CPR will not take you around again. It is known as the dim mak point of no return or neurological shut down. The neurological shut down point when struck will cut off the blood from the brain, cut off the energy that is going to the brain and will cut off the air supply to that person.

Neurological shut down is when you shut the whole nervous system down for a few seconds. Now the body itself will do this sometimes. This happens when a person faints or passes out. The brain will just shut down to see what has happened to sort the mess out and will keep itself shut off to sort the mess out. If nothing happens it will switch itself back on again, usually people recover quite quickly after fainting.

A lot of young inexperienced people are dealing in this practice at present, known as "the American dream ". Personally, I think this sort of thing is very foolish and dangerous. If you make the brain shut itself down involuntary you must be able to bring it back round to consciousness again because when this happens everything will switch off. The brain will switch off so to bring a person back around again, it is how it operates. This practice is highly dangerous and you need to know what you are doing. In the same way you don't mess with electricity or the electric of you home unless you know what you are doing. It is very dangerous to go around practising hitting people on pressure points, as they do now all over the martial art world, for pranks and tricks or an ego boost for the instructor. This is the only reason I mention the Dim Mak principle here as I am talking about healing and not the reverse. Doing this sort of thing just to boost one's own ego is dangerous and wrong and you could cause someone to be brain damaged or brain dead and damaged for life. For instance, if you switch off your VCR in the middle of a taping and if you don't have it tuned in or have the correct buttons pressed then it will not come back on for you.

But in saying all this it can have the reverse effect in healing. Sometimes draining energy from the body is used to cleanse the bodies meridian system so the body will recharge itself again. This can be done on oneself ie see lecture on cultivating chi energy. It is easy to work with energy in the body, not so much with a chair as a chair is not an energy system. It has got energy all right but it is not an energy system. There is nothing to work with. In other words, the chair's energy is vibrating at a different frequency (see lecture on energy dimensions). Although the chair was an energy system at one time ie a tree and you certainly can work with trees and draw energy from them by hugging them or slapping your hands off them or being one with the tree.

☯ A Final note

On a final note, you can pass healing energy on to anyone, for them to accept or not, that's entirely up to them but its better if they ask. If our aura is constantly open, then we need to learn to close it down again through the practice of meditation. When in meditation I advise my students or clients to find their centre of protection to stop other entities or energies getting through. You can't go off all day or night and leave your windows & doors open without the risk of some unwelcome guest coming in so you must close down the energy system i.e. take a cup of tea or go for a walk. We close down the energy system at night when we close our eyes. We move from conscious to a subconscious state or alpha when we close down our energy system. When we lift something heavy we preserve energy by closing the eyes, unfortunately most people will hold their breath. If you hold the breath you will tense the body and tense the lungs and restrict its capabilities. Some people have got the idea that if they hold the breath this will give them more strength; instead it will waste or deplete their whole energy.

All you have to do is close your eyes and twist your waist. Notice in a lot of cultures how a mother lifts her child, she will circle her waist and lift the child with great ease. If she carried the child on the hip this would be totally wrong because she could easily have a damaged hip joint or one leg shorter than the other for the rest of her life, or she could suffer from arthritis. She should carry the child in front of her stomach and drop the energy down through the leg back to the earth. This is why you will be able to lift quite heavy things. And this can be proven by demonstration where you will be able to shift the weight of an object back through your feet back to the earth. However, you must be able to lift the object in the first place and better still if you were doing natural breathing.

Natural breathing, is breathing in through the nose and out through the nose. When you breathe in, the abdominal area will go out and when you breathe out, the abdominal area will go in. This is the natural breath, the way a young baby breathes and the younger the child the more dramatic it is. This is known as diaphragmatic breathing; as you lower and lift the diaphragm naturally and relax it again. Most Westerners breathe in the upper chest causing tension in the lungs and upper body thus restricting the flow of chi. By breathing high up in the chest we are only using 2/3rds or our lungs capacity thus restricting the flow of energy and depleting the strength in our bodies if you are a smoker you are only using 1/3rds of your lung capacity.

Another way of seeing the difference between strength and internal power is when you only use your arm to pick an object up rather than your whole body. This can be see in the practice of taiji i.e. the sweeping lotus kick at the end of the taiji form. The centrifugal and centripetal forces of the waist action generate the power. This has enormous health benefits, as this action causes the chi to circulate from the lower tan-tian to the fingers and toes and back again. Think of an axe man chopping down a tree and a carpenter hammering a nail. The carpenter is only using his triceps and biceps while hammering the nail but the axe man is using the enormous band of waist or abducted muscles to generate the force in chopping down the tree. We have forgotten how to use and how to make use of these muscles in our everyday lives. I think if we used and were taught to use these muscles again in a circular fashion there would be less bad back problems in our society. These muscles are very weak in most people due to a number of factors including the lack of exercise, poor posture and our furniture etc. In lifting a heavy object, you must lift with the power of your legs pushing off the earth and using the circular movement of the waist. To increase this power when you get your object up to navel level you can rest it against your stomach muscles and if you've learned to work the energy system you are able to shift the energy of that object through your legs back to the earth. It is like lifting a bar of steel of the ground. This is very easy for one person, as we know if they lift one end of the steel because the earth will hold the other part of it. This is because the energy of the bar of steel will naturally be direct to the point of contact on the earth. Get two men to lift this same bar of steel and it becomes much easier to do. However, if one of those men go to the centre of the bar it is literally impossible to move because all the energy is being stuck on that earth frequency.

This same principle applies when one is moving a ladder. There will be no effort needed on your part as the weight or energy of the ladder is drawn to the point of contact at that given time to the earth.

I personally think that the pyramids were built on a theory such as this one but of course on a larger scale, I suppose it is all a question of balance. All this I'm sure had nothing to do with technique but was to do with energy and the understanding of being in harmony with the universal energy system. Universal l energy system; ley lines and magnetic fields (see lecture on Earth Ground Frequencies). The same theory applies to energy travelling back to the earth from a greater source to a lesser source. We experience this when we are out for a day, perhaps a day in the city and come home drained. This is because someone out there was

23

taking the energy they needed for themselves. They may not be aware of this but as energy has no conscience it will travel from a greater to a lesser source. It will travel from the healer to the client and on its way on its path of least resistance back to earth, it will pass organs in the body and give them more energy and thus help to stimulate that person's energy and heal them. This happens not because it wants too but because it has too; then so be it.

So taiji and qi-gong as you can gather by now, is indeed very powerful and works on many levels. They have a far greater impact than just physical movements or a little dance round the floor, as indeed one would believe from seeing it for the first time.

Taiji does exceptionally well what it was designed to do. That is to keep you fit and tone and strengthen your body both inside and out. This also creates a relaxed state of mind and takes years of your appearance, a high rate of reward for just 15 minutes of your day, enjoy you taiji.

CHAPTER 2

Healing & Meditation

As in the saying "there are many paths to the top of the mountain, but the view from the top is the same", so healing is manifested in many different ways by different healers. For example, some healers will use different props like bits of linen or cloth, string, a cup of meal, stone, salt as in the church office, water, feathers, sand, oil, prayer, music, colour and touch. These methods are all used in healing and there's a lot more in the many different cultures religions and beliefs.

I am inspired to write this to take away the myth that people have about healing, and to explain the way it works. The thing we must realise about healing, no matter in what shape or form it is given, is to remember that all healing comes from the source and that all healing heals. Now this makes the distinction between healing and curing,

"Is it the bulb that lights the room"? Well we certainly know that the bulb will not light the room unless you put it in the path of the energy flow, as energy travels from a greater source to a lesser source on the path of least resistance. It is the same with channelling chi energy, if you get the right frequency and tap into the correct mind state of total mindfulness you will as a universal law, be allowed to channel this energy. You will not be allowed to channel universal energy for the destruction of mankind. You can only channel universal energy for the good of yourself and others and the planet etc to the highest degree.

All healing comes from the source, the Divine source of wisdom or God, Universal energy or whatever you want to call it. These are just names or labels, the same as healers and healing have many different names such as bio energy healing, vibrational healers, faith healers etc. These are man made names that we put on things to help us understand in some kind of rational way because we have rational minds. All healing, we must remember, comes from the source and healing will never ever take place either physically or mentally or spiritually unless there is compassion between the healer and the client. Words are just words, as the bulb does not light the room.

So in order to tap into the universal source of energy you must have compassion for all life and you will realise this as time goes on - otherwise you would not be interested in this book.

Those that are drawn to these writings are meant to be drawn to them. This is why I am inspired by my spiritual guide (1500 BC) to write this information in simple terms so that you the reader will be able to understand and be guided by this book. This is written to help people to understand and to open up their own abilities to channel energy for the good of others either in music, art, literature or healing. We are all born as equals and some are born with the gift of healing. However, this does not mean that you are born a healer, you become one. In the same way that we are not born good or bad, we become good or bad. Things will happen through meditation or sickness to bring these abilities to the foreground. Because you are sick you get time to think and meditate. The only reason you are sick in the first place, is because you block the flow of chi or universal energy. Some healers cause this to happen, to themselves either by being over religious or over superstitious or by not allowing themselves to have a free spirit.

☯ Meditation and the subconscious

We all have hidden abilities and gifts within us and to open up these abilities we must reach a point of total relaxation and peace. This can only be reached through deep abdominal breathing and relaxation in the practice of meditation. Once we find total relaxation and peace of mind we can open up tremendous doors to the subconscious and beyond. We can learn from meditation that there is much more to life than meets the eye. We can see things much more clearly and in greater depth than we did before we started the meditation practice. However, this will not happen overnight. We must learn to be patient and learn at different stages. Mankind is evolving at a very fast rate today, physically, mentally and spiritually; it is hard to find quiet time for the inner spirit.

We all have meditated at some stage or other in our lives. Maybe we have not been aware of it at the time, perhaps just day dreaming, praying or working outside. I'm sure you have often heard the saying "I'll meditate on that" meaning mainly that when we meditate on something we get results.

Meditation can be explained quite simply; it is like taking a journey on a plane. When going off on a holiday for instance, the journey on the plane could be great but the holiday itself could turn out a disaster. Or vice versa, the holiday itself could be wonderful and you could gain a lot of experience, meet new people and exchange interesting ideas. The plane journey could be terribly frightening, or off putting but when you get there, the holiday could be wonderful. The same applies with meditation. Getting into meditation or a meditative state could be very easy but during the meditation it could turn out to be quite frightening or off putting. Sometimes it could open up things from past lives that we didn't really think we were capable off. On the other hand, it could be the other way around - getting into meditation could be quite difficult but during meditation could be quite peaceful indeed and you could be very happy finding out about other past lives and about your higher self. So this is just one way of explaining meditation, Meditation is when we switch from conscious to subconscious and are still very much aware of what is around us. However, in meditation we are not concerned with what is going on. It is like the state of sleep while staying awake but of course still at rest, Einstein, the greatest physician of all time s referred to meditation as "wakeful rest".

An hour of meditation can be the equivalent of 3 hours sleep. I find that during meditation you can cut down on your consumption of food and be able to wear the same clothing in winter as in summer; being in harmony with nature and the universe. Meditation is where you are present but you are not really bothered with what is going on. You are not concerned with what is going on around you or who that person is or where they are going or coming from. Once you start to think those thoughts you might think they are coming from the shop or something and then you start thinking of your own shopping etc. because the mind is very tricky. You should be able to stay in a state of total mindfulness - that is real meditation. You can switch it on and off at will or in other words you are able to step over the line, the imaginary line between the conscious and the subconscious. You are able to step over from the two consciousnesses and be in complete control. Drug addicts and heavy drinkers do this all the time but the only difference is that they are not in control.

☯ Finding your centre

So you can step over from conscious to subconscious in the matter of thought - not in the matter of seconds but the matter of thought. Thought brings you back and forward by the power of the mind. I have taught this technique to a few of my taiji students and I have learned it myself through trial and error. In the start it brought me to different levels and I must say it scared me at first. The reason for this was that I have always looked for protection from the outside. I built barriers to keep energy out rather than looking for protection from within. I eventually found my centre connection to the spirit within and so that became my protection, energy should flow through you without fear or judgement. Your centre can originate from either your cultural belief or religious belief or any belief, ie pool of energy. When you find your centre then meditation is quite simple no matter what kind of meditation you are involved in. All these big names, transcendental and cosmic meditation, these are just man made names, as indeed, so is meditation, just a word. However, meditation practice is easy to do and very harmless. But on the other hand, if you don't hold your centre in your meditation it can indeed be quite dangerous because the aura or your energy field is open in meditation. It is open to all the other forces or entities of energy around you from other dimensions and they are around you as you will see when we talk about energy dimensions etc. You are open to everything not alone colds and flu's, infections, disease's or adverse weather conditions but you are also open to all other entities of energy from other dimensions. Some of these other entities or energies are not very pleasant and may try to control you or manipulate you, by gaining control of your mind. But if you hold your centre and practice in a nice peaceful state of mind and in harmony with the universal energies then nothing or no one can harm you, as like will draw like. Your aura or energy field will still stay open during meditation but will also be very much protected. There will be a protective shield around you, not a shield alone around you and your aura but there will also be a protective shield around the aura itself. A universal energy shield is what some people call God. So only what is meant to come in will come in and guide you and channel through you. If you keep the aura closed or indeed have a closed mind nothing can come through. You must keep the aura open. When you do meditation in a peaceful state of mind or as someone would say a state of grace, peace and tranquillity etc; well then you draw the right energy to you. It's all a question of vibrations.

☯ Guides and angels

So if you are a healer you will draw other like-minded healers to you, who have passed on to other dimensions. These healers may have evolved to a higher state and may want to come through to you not always in spiritual form of course, but will come through in other forms i.e. thoughts, hot or cold sensations, all kinds of ways to help you here on earth, to carry out your soul journey. You must remember that you are a spirit in a physical body and you are not doing the healing. You are just a channel or are being used to channel this universal energy. Although you can draw of the universal energy and channel it, sometimes that is not enough because your spirit or energy may not be strong enough. You may have to draw off other entities and they most certainly may want to use you as a channel. These are sometimes known to us as our guides or guardian angels or whatever you want to call them. I believe we could have up to 5 or 50 guides at any given time but most of us have just one with helpers or 3 main ones.

So what you are now in this life, you continue to be in the next. If you are a very good person now and living your life in a positive way and living in peace and harmony with the universal energy system you will continue to live in this way in the next life. On the other hand, if you are living your life in a very negative way or doing bad deeds then you will continue to do the same in the next life. In passing from this dimension to the next, like will draw like.

So, in meditation, you will open up the doors to the universal energy system. You will tap into channels that you never thought you had. You will become conscious of abilities, which you had locked away in the subconscious. You will be able to stay in a meditative state for quite some time perhaps 1 to 2 hours or even longer. In meditation, time has no meaning as you are outside time and space. Some people have the gift of travelling in the astral body or *esoteric* body in other dimensions outside time and space but this will be discussed later on in the chapter on energy dimensions.

☯ Channelling energy back to the earth

When you are in a meditative state you are being channelled by the universal energy system, you are being healed yourself. Every organ and individual cell is being channelled with this life given force of energy (chi). It is helping you to evolve physically, mentally and spiritually and getting rid of any toxins or negative blockages in your body. These toxins are channelled out through the soles of your feet back to the earth to be purified. The energy underneath the ground or on the earth's surface is positive and the energy above the earth is negative energy. So the energy must go back to the ground again to the point of least resistance to be purified and rise again and change state to spirit, just as the chi rises and changes state in the body to Zen or spirit. Sometimes too, you will have energies lingering in buildings just as an old pair of shoes gathers moss a lot of stagnant or negative energy. In the same way a pool of negative energy may have gathered beneath the grounds of the building or near the building. The negative energy may not actually be contained within the building itself though it may have some negative charges in it from the negative thoughts that people left there. As the law of physics states energy cannot be destroyed, it can only be transformed, so there may be small changes of energy in the stonework or furniture etc, but mainly in the earth.

So our job as healers is not just to heal the physical or spirit but also to heal the earth and channel the stagnant energy back to the earth. This is the highest level of any healer. First you heal yourself, then you heal others, then you teach others to heal and lastly you heal the earth. We channel the negative energy back to the earth to be purified and it changes state, rises to spirit and becomes one with the universal energy system.

If you give out a negative thought, it will just bounce back on what I call the universal mirror and it will come back on you. But if we give out positive thoughts it will do likewise, because the natural law of the universe is, that what you give out will come back not once but ten-fold. This is the natural law of the universe and nothing or no one can change it, it's simple but powerful.

☯ It is how we live that is important

So when we are in meditation we are in total peace and tranquillity with ourselves, with others and all things around us. We can stay in this state for as long as necessary and go into it at will. This is the door or key to eternal glory because all it is at the end of the day is in your mind. Whatever you have ie wealth or money or material things, they as we know, will not stay with you. The best swindlers in this world have not yet managed to take a single penny from this dimension to the next. But your memory, your personality, your knowledge and wisdom are important and go with you. So what you are now you always will be. Some cultures got lost in this somewhere along the way as they got so involved in reincarnation that they completely stopped bothering or doing things while here on earth. This is wrong, as you just can't wait around for the final day to come. You must get up and get on with it and stay prepared for the passing, (death) each day, from one dimension to the next. That's the bottom-line - the rest will make no difference.

If you are a terrible worrier or if you are a so-called grabber of material wealth, in 50 or 100 years' time it will make no difference. But what will make a difference is the way you live your life. This doesn't mean that you have to go around like a saint as these are few and far between; again a saint is only a name. It is a name we put on someone who is in harmony with all things and at peace with their own mind. You don't have to worry about where the next mortgage is coming from; your guides will look after you. In saying this, you must make an effort, as a little struggle is a must.

We all have guides. We may think that we are guides ourselves. Some of us call ourselves sifu or master or sensi, these are just egotistical names that we put on ourselves to make us feel more important than those we guide. These are just names or titles and if you died with a title attached to your name (sir or doctor) or some name to this effect well that title will die with you. The only thing you carry with you is your name, your first name, personality and knowledge - the rest is unimportant. What you are now, you continue to be that forever. What you were when you were two years of age, though you may not remember, you were still you, when you were ten years of age, you were still you, and before that you were still you. At whatever age you pass over you will still be you, you will never change. So what you are worried about now or are concerned with will not matter in 50 or 100 years' time. However, this does not mean that you should lie around and do nothing. You must get up and make an effort because nothing will happen if we don't make an effort. On the other hand, if we worry and try too hard we block everything (the flow of energy or universal chi). So we must learn to stay relaxed, be at peace and live everyday as it comes and be content in the moment of here and now, as there is no such thing as the past or the future. The future is the present moment of another time that will be now and the pasts is the present moment of another time that was now. Life is eternal; either in a physical body or out of a physical body, life is continuous and eternal. There is just the present; the eternal here and now and we are living in all 3 dimensions at the same time, in the past, present and future. When we pass on we may be able to stay in the 4th and 5th dimension or higher but here and now we can only live in the third dimension and that is the only thing that should concern you in your practice of meditation. However, in the continuous practice of meditation you will be able to reach the forth and fifth dimension frequency and indeed the planet at present is moving between the forth and fifth dimension frequencies. Evidence of this can be seen all over the world as the old hard ways of the past are going and more peaceful relaxed ways are approaching. More and more souls are evolving through the heart Chakra by compassion and this is having an affect on our planet, because without love and compassion nothing can evolve.

Meditation can be done in many different ways ie, taiji or qi-gong or The Seven Set Practice etc. or similar practice. It doesn't have to be The Seven Set Practice. A similar form of meditation will do such as prayer, chanting, singing, colour, the use of colour, and the use of candle and flames etc. Any system or doctrine that will enhance the flow of energy and keep the Chakras spinning and healthy is fine.

These methods will bring us to the same mind state as there are many paths to the top of the mountain but the view from the top is still the same. So meditation is a tranquil, peaceful state of mind, that's all it is.

CHAPTER 3

Energy Dimensions

In all seven dimensions known to the author, the energies are vibrating at seven different frequencies and all are related to the seven Chakras, the seven auras or magnetic field around the body. These are all governed and controlled by the laws of the universe and are part of the whole cosmic state. All these vibrations are connected to the five earthly elements, i.e. wood, fire, earth, metal and water. The same connection is present in the five vowels and the five seasons in oriental terms and in the meridians in the human body (see introduction).

We are between the heavens and the earth and in a manner of speaking, heaven equals breath and earth equals food and water and the esoteric energy is between the two. We keep them connected and together by just being here and plants and trees help also with this connectivity. As I said in the chapter on taiji (tai chi) think of this great big thing stuck onto your feet. This is only one way that the earth gets charged with cosmic energy and it is how we humans, plants and animals get charged or draw on the earth's energy.

However, the earth gets charged with cosmic forces not only through the channel of plants, trees and flowers etc. but also directly from the storms, thunder, lightening, wind, rain, hail, snow and of course sunlight.

Energy travels to and fro all the time, in all these ways, helping with the very existence of earthly life.

We also get solar energy directly or indirectly through the food we eat. We get this energy by eating either directly from the earth, i.e. fruit and vegetables or eating meat or drinking the milk from animals that get their food directly from the earth.

All of this food is turned into energy to help us grow and develop and anything we don't want is sent back to the earth. In other words, anything that is of no value to us after it has served its purpose is let back to the earth. Eventually, when we no longer need our physical body it too goes back to the earth. Our energy however is transformed to spirit or Zen and goes back to join with the universal energies to be at one. In doing so, we must travel through the different dimensions; this may take many life times to reach, who knows? It is all one great learning process, to help us to find our Divine path and destiny. Everything goes back to the earth when we pass over to the other dimensions, but our subconscious which has three separate parts i.e. mind, spirit and soul goes outside time and space and finds enlightenment. Before it reaches total spiritual awareness however, it has to learn and perform tasks on the other dimensions, to help the rest of us that are on the same journey but are at different levels. In all of this, lessons are learned both here on earth and on other dimensions.

A lot of the time people from the 3 rd dimension, pass on to the 4th and 5th dimensions but usually it is the 4th dimension. However, some souls stay on the earth or close to the astral plane, as sometimes these souls don't realise that they have passed over and sometimes we here on earth grieve too much and they cannot pass on.

☯ Astral Travel

Many people will have this experience here while still in their physical body i.e. astral travel or near death experience. Astral travel is different to mind projection or remote viewing but all of these disciplines will help you to do astral travelling providing fear does not get in the way. The mind is tricky and you must protect your energy field or aura. Remote viewing and mind projection can be of great benefit in absent healing i.e.

where you heal people from a distance by just thought as thought will travel anywhere without limits, (see absent healing)

Chi projection or mind projection on the other hand, is where you simply go into a meditative state and project your chi or energy to another person, place or dimension. Remote viewing is where you use your mind in a meditative state to visualise yourself being in that place or with that person. This is a wonderful technique to use in absent healing and nowadays; it is getting quite popular in police training in the U.S.A.

Astral travel, on the other hand, is where you can actually be with that person or in that place and your physical body remains where it is. The reverse of this skill is bilocation, where you can be in two places at the one time, an ability that's sought after by many spiritual practitioners but reached by only a few.

☯ The Esoteric Body

The body has several outer bodies or esoteric layers of energy fields and these are all shadows of the physical. We know that the physical body is made up of molecules i.e. carbon, hydrogen, oxygen and nitrogen which make up a single atom. This is what is known as matter. The esoteric body is not matter but as the name suggests is esoteric, just like you have ice, water and steam.

Sometimes by will or not by will the esoteric body can leave the physical body and go to the astral plane, this is why it is known as the astral body.

This is achieved by raising one's vibrations to a different frequency through relaxed breathing techniques in meditation. This is achieved in the same way as we change the vibrations of ice to water, to steam, and back to water and ice again. When the esoteric body leaves the physical at the time of passing, it breaks off its life force meridian; psychics can see this as a silver cord. In astral travel one can leave the physical, or the esoteric body can leave the physical and travel on the astral plane.

The only thing that is keeping us from doing so is fear i.e. fear of the unknown. But if we keep our centre and stay relaxed then nothing or no entity can harm us or will indeed want to harm us. They will only guide us ever further on our journey of life.

At first when people are practising they get so far, and as they feel their bodies getting lighter they tense up and are yanked back to the physical. The esoteric or guides will always look after the physical and keep unwanted entities of energies away. This is not the same as sleep or dreaming though in sleep we may travel on the astral plane without being aware of it. However, in a near death experience we will be aware of it and we will be close to the astral plane and the 4th and 5th dimensions. In the case of passing over most beings stay in the 4th dimension until such time as they realise where they come from, what they are doing there and when they are leaving to go further on their journey of total spiritual awareness.

Many souls will choose to stay on the 4th and 5th dimensions to help other souls to evolve to the 5th and 6th dimensions before moving on. It does not mean that when you pass over you will know everything. No, because whatever you are now you continue to be. If your mind is not open and at peace at the moment of passing, and long before, you could find yourself on the same merry-go-round. Some may take one lifetime and some could take a thousand of life times. It is one great learning process and not to be taken lightly.

However, all of this does not mean that we should not enjoy life. Life is a wonderful gift and remember that what we give out we get back ten fold.

This is the law of the universe and nothing or no one can change it.

☯ Astral Travelling and healing

So here on earth other entities will work with us and through us in the many gifts and talents we have - not just healing, as every gift is special and every one is special. They will also work very hard in helping us to find our higher-self or the God within but they will not interfere with our free will as this is another and most important law of the universe in the Divine scheme of things. One can get to these dimensions in the practice of meditation i.e. being outside time and space as so often happens during a healing session. Sometimes during a healing session, a person or clients esoteric body leaves the physical to have healing done on another dimension and this is manifested in the physical, of total relaxation, almost to the point of sleep.

Again to understand this, think of ice, water and steam and then take into account things like emotions, thoughts, words, deeds and actions etc.

In healing, the vibrations of the body are raised by the healer's channels of universal energies. This may happen to such an extent, that the client will have the feeling of total peace and harmony with themselves and others and with all things around them. They will have the feeling of being in all dimensions and yet just being in the one dimension. In those moments, there are no fears or worries, just peace and fulfilment of the spirit, unity with their higher self and the universal energy.

☯ The Importance of Meditation

Some of us will experience this feeling of peace and relaxation in meditation and in daydreaming but not in sleep or dreaming. In dreaming we may travel through a lot of dimensions but because there is a memory lapse when we awake out of sleep, or out of the alpha state, we forget our dreams and even when we try to remember them nothing makes sense. So the best way of seeing into other dimensions or other worlds is through the practice of meditation, where you are aware but not concerned or frightened, but just at peace. This is, what I believe, should be the feeling of passing over or passing on. This is why it is important to have peace of mind all the time but especially in the time of passing from one dimension to the next. Otherwise the journey could be a very difficult one, but help is always available, we only have to ask.

When we go on a journey we prepare ourselves and in passing over we prepare the esoteric body by finding peace. Every journey we undertake, the physical body goes with us except in the passing from this dimension to the next, because as we know, we no longer need the physical body in the next dimension.

☯ Meditation and Astral Travelling

We are outside time and space and we can go anywhere (in our mind) as we wish by thought. However, if were on a lower dimension i.e. 4th we cannot go to the 5th until we progress further. We can however, manifest in any shape or form and vibrate on a higher or lower frequency.

Many souls ie mediums, gifted psychics and healers, can pick up these vibrations from other dimensions that are on the same frequency. We have lost these gifts to mankind by our cultural and religious conditioning of the past. We were told that practising these gifts was of the occult. Surely helping others cannot be of the occult, and what is the occult but a name man made to keep us within the boundaries of good and evil. This book clearly states that there is no such thing as good and evil. "Thinking makes it so". This may be a blunt statement and somewhat confusing as one might ask the question here what about heaven or hell? Again one must remember that the concept of heaven and hell is man made, and as my spiritual guide says "as man thinks so shall he be, as he sows so shall he reap" what you give out you get back. This is how man determines his own salvation although according to the Divine plan every soul will reach full spiritual awareness in the fullness of time. Everyone has free will and whatever he / she chooses then so be it. That is why these gifts are coming back round again, to help mankind reach full spiritual awareness. No doubt this time they will be taken with a much more open minded view and hopefully man will awaken to the great spiritual powers of the universe, that are within his/her grasp.

☯ Seven Different Frequencies

In all seven dimensions there are seven different frequencies and vibrations i.e. talking, singing, praying, meditation, chi projection and mind projection. These vibrations are usually reached through deep and relaxed breathing skills, which raise the energy to Zen or spirit. The acts of breathing, contemplation, visualisation and imagination are the key points for wholesome living. This keep one's energy flowing freely through the body and in this way keeps a balance between positive and negative charges and therefore keeps us healthy. In other words, we can take control of our health, free health if you like. When something goes wrong you can fix it. You have the power; the power is within your mind.

When the energy enters your body at the time of conception it is fused by both your father and mother and is sacred i.e. "when two or more come together in my name". Before birth this energy is pure but in passing from one dimension to another at birth, a soul may have chosen to take with it a trade mark i.e. big feet, cancer, blindness, healing and so on, the list is endless. It will choose these things to learn lessons and to teach others lessons. This is the Divine plan i.e. destiny steps in. Sometimes too, cultural and religious beliefs and social conditioning etc block the pure energy. So now it is not as pure as it was, and there is no balance, so disease and sickness enter the new body. This happens to let that person know that they must change and to remind that person who they really are and their soul purpose. This is why a lot of sick people change their attitude to life over night. A person may also be sick in order to change the lives of those closest to them or even to change the lives of those who are looking after them.

This is all too often misunderstood and people treat sickness like a curse. It is not a curse; this is how we learn and evolve spiritually, mentally and physically. We learn lessons so we do not find ourselves back on the same merry-go-round, of the wheel of incarnation. How would we like to go to all the effort of getting ready for a holiday only to find that in five hours later we were still sitting in the same place? We would be fed up indeed. Life here is like an airport terminal where we stop off on our journey to get the next flight. If we have lost our passport or tickets we won't get off in the first place and we won't get back either, we won't get back to higher-self and find our true self and destiny. The ticket I talk about here is an open, calm and relaxed mind.

☯ An Open Mind

Through many years of practising meditation and living many life times we can transcend to the higher frequencies or (higher-self) and come back as often as we wish. We can do this as quickly as thought, by the power from within i.e. the mind, by raising the vibrations. So it is not important how much material wealth or money one has but it is important that we open the doors in our mind and not to have a closed mind. Certainly we must live in a home or place of shelter and mow the lawns etc. For now, we have money as a means of exchange and we put our money to good use. As long as we do not loose sight of where we are i.e. the earth, and most importantly who we are and the journey we are undergoing, then there's no problem. Now this does not mean that we should be

41

waiting around all day for something spiritual to happen. If we did that, we would lose all our gifts and talents. We would get nothing done and receive nothing in return. What you give out you get back or what goes around comes around. Kneeling down all day long will get us nowhere and we would probably end up with arthritic joints. We must get up and do something and take responsibility for our own actions, as the saying goes "a little struggle is a must".

Now do not get me wrong here; there is nothing wrong with kneeling down as long as it's done in meditation i.e. with the right frame of mind, attitude and free spirit. I find that most religious groups and organisations have got the wrong idea when they separate themselves from the centre i.e. God and then they tell their followers that its all up to God.

If we leave everything up to God or your so called God, then good chances are we will not do anything ourselves. You might argue the point here that we have all got free will and yes that's true; and it's this choice of our free will, thoughts, words and actions that will determine the world we create for ourselves to live in.

☯ A Balanced Life

What I find with most religious people or groups is that they work hard with the spirit and there's nothing wrong with that. However, they sometimes forget about the physical. On the other hand, some people over work the physical and forget about the spirit or their connection to spirit so therefore there is no balance. We must be able to reach a balance between the two. You can't take a group of males or females and stick labels on them and stop them from using their life given energy i.e. their sexual energy. If you do that you will end up with a disaster. We cannot put on fancy robes, labels or belts and then think that we are in control or have control of the universal energy. No one is any better than the next. We're all equal no matter what race, colour, religion or creed This kind of practice has been done once too often in the past in so many religions, cultures, beliefs and practices and look at the results.

So to finish, as long as we are careful with our thoughts, words, deeds and actions and stay in harmony with the universal energy then we can enjoy life as life is for living.

CHAPTER 4

Life is for Living

We are living in a physical body, in a physical world in this dimension; therefore, we should enjoy our physical pleasures as well as our spiritual side. Life is for living, for giving and receiving. Getting too stuck down or taking life too seriously is of no use to anyone. Waiting around all the time for things to happen or longing to have spiritual gifts i.e. psychic abilities i.e. seeing ghosts, spirits and other entities. Seeing these things is not at all important as all of this depends on one's progress. It is not a question of sitting around for hours meditating or doing The Seven Set Practice in this book or doing similar training. Not at all, it is all a question of how you live your life. If you are not truly spiritual then these gifts will not be rewarded to you, no matter how spiritually advanced you appear to be.

The mind has many levels and the soul is just one of these. The soul has infinite energies and all energies have different levels. In spiritual matters everyone develops in their own time and in many lifetimes. The sum total of what you have been, good and bad is what you are now. This makes the subject of passed lives complicated. Indeed, it is better left alone because genetic memories become mixed up with our own mind memories and it is very difficult to separate our memories from previous lives from those of our ancestors. We all have to live our lives while paying for our ancestors' actions and the damage they have done to their psychic. Everything you do is recorded and the efforts you make will all be recorded i.e. "every hair on your head is counted ". However, in saying this everyone has free will and choice in this matter.

☯ Energy Dimensions

When spirits or people pass on and have not advanced spiritually or not given up on material wealth and earthly things then they are drawn closer to the 3rd dimension. They are drawn into a pool of spinning energy. This happens because of their mind state in passing "as man thinks so shall he be." They are drawn closer to the alpha plane, where the energies become denser and more physical and because of earthly desires and weaknesses, these energies are fused again when a male and female come together in the act of love for procreation.

Now these souls are then trapped in this dimension and are reborn again so that lessons can be learned. Again this is all very difficult to understand while in the physical plane and in the physical body.

However, this is not always the case as higher entities or souls will sometimes choose to be born, to bring about evolution and to work a plan to balance everything out.

On the other hand, some souls are too lazy to advance to a higher spiritual level because of their longing for earthly things. They grow so attached to the earth and lurk around on the alpha plane in old dwellings etc. This is because part of their mind energy is in a time trap. Some memory or event of earthly existence will bring them back to this dimension for a short time until the old memory has passed. This is why some ghosts and spirits are seen at certain times and places.

If you do come across an entity of this nature just remember, that they will be just as surprised to see you, as you are to see them. All you may do is ask it to move on by the power of your thought. However, they may wait around until a spiritual healer can set their minds free of disturbing thoughts and give them peace at last. There are people on earth guided towards these tasks and the rest of us should leave well enough alone. It is not a healthy practice to deliberately set about contacting the deceased or ghosts and spirits etc. This I assure you, is not good either for yourself or for the other entities and can only lead to confusion and sickness of the mind.

To put it simply, it is like invading someone's mind. You live in your world and they live in their parallel world and we are all linked to the universal time structure in Divine plan of things. Just as here on earth, each of us live in this world i.e. 3rd dimension, but we also live in little worlds of our own, ie our minds.

☯ Spirit World

If you want to contact someone who has passed over, all you have to do is to sit quietly and think of that person and immediately you will be linked up to that person's mind dimension. This is very complicated and is far better left alone. If the dead want to contact us they will find a way. They usually do so through our old memories i.e. old photographs of themselves while they were here on earth or inspirations of one kind or another i.e., voice intuition etc. In the spirit world no stone is left unturned and the dead spirit will go to every length to sort things out. If for instance a soul leaves this world in a violent death which is a violent shock to ones energy system then they will not move on, until everything is in order, no matter how long it takes. This is another reason why spirits hang around. They will hang around to finish what they came for without having to enter into a physical body on the earthly plane.

This all depends on their mind state and how far they have advanced spiritually, as there's no such thing as time in this dimension. Only then are they glad to move on and 'give up the ghost', as this is not healthy for the soul. We must move on and find our true destiny.

Dimensions are like states of minds or thoughts that we do not change overnight, even though sometimes it may seem that way. This takes many years, and indeed could take many life times. Everyone is evolving, all in their own good time on different levels and there are many levels, many possibilities, many realities and many truths and you have to fine your own truth.

Some ghosts or spirits may not want to be there and some may not even know that they have passed on because of a violent shock to their body's energy system i.e. suicide, accident or other violent death. Also many souls think that they have to protect some part of the earth's energy i.e. houses or favourite places, especially if they were the household figure in that house when they were on earth. They also may find that they are very much at peace in the earth's sacred places. Again if you feel that you are quite sensitive to these energies, just remember that they can do you no harm and do not want to, as like attracts like. However, ask them to move towards the light as there are other higher entities waiting to help them, but this is all very much like healing and healers. You can't force your gift on anyone no more than the higher spirits can force you towards the light. This is where a spiritual healer or guide on this dimension can work best and guide them towards the light.

We all have free will and everything happens in its own good time. As each of us are on different paths and will reach our reward whatever that may be, it is entirely up to us the way we live our lives, so enjoy life; life is for living.

☯ Ghosts and spirits

Ghosts are entities of energy brought about by a thought or memory of a mind state of that person as they remember themselves as they were here on earth. Because they are easier to see in dim or dark conditions this makes them all the more frightening. As I said that they are probably just as surprised to see you, as you are to see them. They are usually in a mind trap, which is known in some religions as purgatory. Spirit, on the other hand, is that entity of energy that has found its spiritual path and knows its path and destiny. Spirits are on a different level and are not in a mind trap. They usually show themselves the way they remember themselves to have been when they had a physical body here on earth i.e. usually their last incarnation.

Some spirits have not even been born yet, as their time is not right. Some still indeed have part of their journey to continue to reach the higher self of true spiritual awareness.

They will still have duties to do, to help them evolve like organising things on the earthly plain. They help all sorts of gifted people here one earth, working in harmony with the universal energy, for the Divine plan of things. They work best away from the alpha plane, or on the 3rd lay line meridian of the earth (see lecture on earth lay lines).

Ghosts on the other hand stay close to the alpha plane, and will not move on until everything is in order. Some will choose to be reborn again, in the hope that they can make a better job of living the next time round, with the lessons they have learned.

Though some indeed are too lazy to be reborn again and just hang around making a nuisance of themselves. In spirit world as we call it, souls are looked after, usually by a family member, grand parent, aunt, uncle or some one whom they regarded as their friend back on earthly life. It is the same as when we are born, here a close member of the family, usually our parents, look after us. We are given lessons to learn, as knowledge is the only way we can progress spiritually. Some people may have this kind of experience in an O B E experience (out of the body or a near death experience). Some people call this astral travel.

☯ Higher Spiritual Beings and Guides

Spirits are guided by higher spiritual beings and are not in a mind trap. They can move from one level to another. However, they travel within their own level or below it but they can't travel above their own level. Now this does not mean that these souls have to be reborn again in another earthly life. This all depends on what efforts they have made on other dimensions.

However, the higher spirit, which may or may not have a physical body, or indeed have one for thousands of years, can move freely in all dimensions. They are as what's known as the higher Masters or ascended Masters.

These higher beings choose, of their own free will, to come back to the earthly plane for the benefit of mankind to help them to progress spiritually, as this is one of the lowest forms of life in the universe. So they will choose to come here on earth and because of their divine love and wisdom, see all life as equal and see God in each of us. They will enter into this world carrying great gifts of balance, wisdom and knowledge to help us here on earth to evolve spiritually. Sometimes they will choose to be very sick to keep them earthed or grounded (see lecture on rooting), as to be saintly here on earth is not an easy task. So some souls can only stay for a short time. However, not all sick people are of a higher nature but because of their sickness they will learn the true values of life and will advance spiritually from their experience. There are also spirits around acting as our guides and again they may or may not have a physical body. They can take on any shape or form that they think might benefit the soul they are guiding.

This will explain why some mediums see people's spiritual guides in the form of powerful animals or gentle birds etc. But this goes much deeper than this and because of our weak minds; this is too difficult to understand while in the physical body. Some people may have more than one guide or guardian angel, as some religions call them. They are with us all the time both here on earth and in our passing, helping us but not interfering with our free will.

☯ Mind States and Guides

It is only when we find peace within ourselves that we become attuned to them in inspiration. This level of attunement may take many life times. Whether you are aware of it or not you have your guide or guides (guardian angels) both here on earth and on the other dimensions. You may even have acted as their guide when they were here on the physical plane, who knows?

Ghosts and spirits and poltergeists i.e. (mischievous spirits) are of both sides of a coin. They work on the level of their mind state and are attracted to our minds' energy by our mind state, to influence us in some way. So if we have negative thoughts and bad feelings towards our fellow men we will attract negative and nasty spirits from the lower vibrations. On the other hand, if we have positive, kind and loving thoughts, we will attract good and kind loving spirits from the higher vibrations – it's as simple as that. There is no such thing as good or bad energy - there is just the absence of light. Everything in this universe is governed by positive and negative charges and we must find a balance. One way of doing this is to keep within the laws of the universe.

Energy is neither good nor bad but it is the mind state we use it at that matters. The laws of the universe say that like will attract like and that what we give out comes back, not once but ten times over. So remember to stay in control of your mind state, your thoughts and you will have no problem in finding your balance.

☯ 'The Paranormal'

Young people today are searching and looking for their spiritual path. Sometimes their search will lead them to dabble in the paranormal and in the practice of séance and Ouija board. One has to be careful with these practices as those with weaker minds could draw on the lower entities of similar mind states. This is very dangerous not only to the mind that attracts the spirit but also to everyone in the group, as energy will travel from a greater source to a lesser source be that source negatively or positively charged. This will depend on the mind state of the person or even the mind state of the entire group at the time of practising. Doing the Ouija board for a bit of fun may appear harmless but because of our human weakness and our lust for power, what happens is often dangerous. Sticking our noses into the realms of the spirit dimension with little or no regard for these dimensions or for our inner spirit makes this a dangerous pastime and in my eyes should be left alone.

I've been asked many times whether there could be any harm in contacting good spirits in this way. My answer is always the same. If the dead want to contact us they will do so in some other way and in their own good time. We should not contact them or even attempt to do so. Most of those who pass on to the other dimensions are no longer attracted to this world or to its desires. They are far too busy adapting to their new surroundings and getting on with their lives and would not be bothered in contacting us. Now we would be far better off to get on with our lives instead of wasting valuable time sitting around having séances etc. Their lives are as real to them now as they were when they were in the physical world and as real to them as our lives are to us. The only difference is that our lives are material and physical while their lives are esoteric and spiritual. Whether they find themselves in a place of peace or turmoil, this all depends on their mind state at the moment of passing. This is how we determine our own salvation.

☯ Knowledge and Imagination

Do not waste time; expand your mind to the great spiritual powers of the universe and to the abundance of knowledge that goes with it, as knowledge is the only wealth in the other dimensions. So the more the mind is open the more knowledge can come through and the greater chance one has of reaching the higher self and the higher dimensions. An open mind helps, so you do not find yourself back on the same merry-go-round and back on the same section of the incarnation cycle. An open calm and peaceful mind helps us to reach our final destiny in the divine plan of things. We should live our lives and enjoy life in whatever dimension we find ourselves in. Just remember that you are honoured to have a physical body in the first place. You are above all other species because you have the power of your mind through the wonderful magical world of your imagination. When you were a child, you used your imagination and it is our task to become like little children again and keep the imagination alive. By keeping the child within, one will have the passport and the key to eternal glory. "Unless you become like little children you will not enter the Kingdom of Heaven'. How many of us truly understand this? Imagination is the greatest gift of all, and for all times. I hope that by using this gift wisely, it will bring us closer to the force that surrounds each and every one of us, by finding again the child within.

CHAPTER 5
Investing in Loss & Rooting

There are three main sources of energy in the body and here I will attempt to show you some ways of regaining your energies, by sacrifices of one kind or another. The Chinese and other ethnic cultures call this investing in loss or in other cultures and religious bodies it is known as penance.

The three main energy sources in the human body are Number one, sexual or survival, Number two, digestion and Number three, work or mental thought and through the incorrect use of these we deplete the bodies energy system. These are known in some other cultures as the eight bits of life. In our youth we burned up about a third of our life's sexual or survival energy by running around, climbing trees etc. As young adults we procreate and have children or as most people say we have sex and once again we deplete our energy. However, this is the way we are made, how else would we evolve? We are just doing what nature intended. However, as we get older and realise that this energy is precious, we learn to control our wants and desires rather than waste our energy through selfish living. Instead we should use it for greater things and this is why in meditation and similar practices we regain the life force energy that we have lost.

Confusion and frustration are the results of suppressing this natural energy. I believe that this confusion and frustration is the so-called devil of our times. This can be seen in many groups and organisations in today's world. Organisations can be harmful if one is not allowed to express their free will. One may wonder why I bother to write these lectures in the first place but I'm inspired to write this stuff to help people regain their life force energy and to cultivate their internal energies by investing in loss.

Investing in loss is where you do something for others and want nothing in return. Perhaps cut the grass for someone or put a friend or stranger up for the night, any help you can give another person, however small, for no payment or charge. This is why most healers have no fee but will accept a gift of one kind or another.

If money or material wealth becomes the main issue then, the true meaning of healing goes because you cannot put a price on universal energy. However, at the same time healers are ordinary men and women and they all have to live. So in a nutshell investing in loss is making small sacrifices to gain greater things spiritually.

☯ Rooting and Earth Spirits

"You must sink before you rise, and rise before you sink"

Before we do any exercises in cultivating chi energy or channelling energy we must first of all get rooted. Ever since the beginning of time, man was told to be rooted or grounded, man has never been told to be aired. A lot of people think that looking up while meditation is rooting them. How silly this is as one only has to look at a tree to see how rooted it is and how well balanced it is with everything around it. Cut of its branches and its roots are no longer needed and cut of its roots and its branches are no longer needed and the tree will eventually die.

Man is both physical and esoteric and he has esoteric or energy roots to keep him in contact with the earth. This is very important for him, physically, mentally and spiritually but sadly a lot of people have lost their roots to the earth. The main reason that we have lost our roots is simply by becoming too materialistic. Man has basically destroyed the earth by putting on shoes in the first place.

This was his first step away from nature and he went on to create concrete jungles of towns and cities because he got too concerned with material wealth. This took him further away from nature and eventually away from his centre or higher self or God. Not everyone who moves into the bigger towns or cities lose their roots but this is just given here as an example of how man lost his way with nature and his contact with the earth. Certainly we must live in the bigger towns and cities and work there, but as long as we do not let this work be the focal point and make a God of material things we can hold onto our roots. We could also live in the country and lose our roots and many sadly do, even though nature is all around them. Again this is because they has falling into the trap of material wealth, using drugs and any other means to fatten up their stock, making them rich surely, but making them poor physically, mentally and spiritually. So man is lost in the trap of the more he has, the more he wants. If he could only wake up and realise that he will not need one single penny in the other dimensions.

So it does not matter where you live your life but it is important how you live it. If you were brought up in the country and for some reason you had to move to a bigger town or city, then it would be easy to loose your contact with the earth. That is why a lot of city folk are taking up some form of relaxing therapy i.e. yoga, meditation, taiji, and other martial arts forms. The martial arts are the more common practice, because of our crime rate in our towns and cities, though there is a lot less crime in today's world than there was in the time of 1500 BC. But sadly man has forgotten who he is and has forgotten where he is. If man still had his roots and was in harmony with nature, there would be no crime, no need for martial training not even to keep sickness away because there would be no sickness. But we do not live in a perfect world and were never meant to live in a perfect world. If this were so, then earthly existence would not be necessary. Crime, sickness, wars, persecution and conflict are all there for a purpose. This is all part of the Divine plan to help us reach full spiritual awareness. This is why no man has the right to pass judgement on another man, no matter how bad his actions appear to be. Every soul will determine their salvation in the fullness of time. Through these experiences we become closer to earth and more in harmony with nature and our fellow men. This is natures' way of balancing everything out so for every up there is a down and for every full belly there is an empty one. So, to keep us in contact with spiritual values, we use what is under our feet and we become more rooted, and more in control of our destiny.

☯ Rooting and Nature Spirits

In grounding our own energy or cosmic energy back to the earth we get rooted to the earth and we can then draw on the earth's energies. This is nature's way of keeping the positive and negative charges flowing freely in and around our bodies, so that we can have a much more balanced life and be in control of our wants and desires. This is achieved by the power of the mind. Through visualisation and imagination, we come closer to nature and to the earth spirits or entities and they in turn will help us because that is their job from their dimension. But if we are not in harmony with them we cannot get help in the first place. We then lose our roots and our contact with mother earth and all sorts of things start to happen. We may experience physical or emotional pain or mental torture of one kind or another. These things can happen at any time in our lives if we are living separate from spirit or have a broken spirit.

Long ago in this country Ireland and in Eastern Europe, people had close contact with nature and the earth's spirits. In Pre Christian time or Pagan times in Ireland man was dependent on nature for his food, clothes, shelter etc. He was so dependent on nature and so close to it that he went to the point of worshipping it as God. I think the only mistake he made was to put one in front of the other. There was the God of fire, the God of water, the God of earth etc whereas they are all part of the one entity of energies that is Divinity, which is God. These people worshipped the earth spirits and had the greatest respect for them and thankfully some groups still do to the present day. Even in the penal days in Ireland, the holy host was buried under the blackthorn bush for fear that the enemy would find it, as they were not allowed to read mass. So they turned to nature once more and trusted the blackthorn to keep the sacred host safe or were they asking the blackthorn spirit to do it for them? At that time man was caught in the battle of religion and superstition and some were so confused in their own beliefs of what was Pagan or Christian, (as one mans superstition is another mans religion). However, the old school of thought won the day. Man was still very much in harmony with the earth spirits and in total contact with the earth. He was not afraid of the power of the earth, as he ancestrally knew that he was part of it and that it was there to help him not just for the more obvious reasons for food and shelter but to keep him in awareness of spirit and of spiritual values.

☯ Rooting and the church

Because of the domineering power of the church up to this time, the ordinary good living people became more and more afraid of the earth and nature spirits and over time, they lost their contact with the earth and also lost their faith and trust in nature. They have not regained this contact since. However, in the last decade or so, man is coming back to earth and living more in harmony with it, by having more respect for nature, plants, animals, and his fellow man etc. For thousands of years they had been told that this kind of practice was evil and if they wanted anything they should come to the church. The church was to be where their spiritual needs (healing of all kinds of sickness and diseases) would be taken care of. You may recall early in this book I said that the power of healing came from the earth. Then if this is so, how then did the church have the power, when it was so strict on the people, by not allowing them to work with nature and its spirits etc?

Those who had the healing power never lost their contact with the earth and because they were living good lives through their vocations, e.g. as a priest, they had the gift of healing simply, because they were rooted (or grounded).

Now, a lot of the high status clergy and dignitaries within the church were jealous of anyone having this gift, when they could not grasp it themselves. They did not approve of these types of healings, i.e. the salt offerings and other forms of healings that went on outside the church itself. This created an enormous gap between church and priest or healer that lead some of them to total frustration, and because of this, the priests were not grounded. This sadly has caused some members of the church to over step their positions of power by controlling others and sadly it goes on today. However, I'm glad to see that things are changing and barriers are coming down every day and that this gap is narrowing once more between religions and spirituality. Now not all of them use their energy in a negative way towards others. Some got hooked on addictions mostly alcohol and because of these human habits, they felt that they had to do some sort of penance, usually after every healing, and indeed some healers think the same way today. They think by doing some form of suffering or taking on someone's pain that the healing will be more powerful. My spiritual guides tell me that the way of the cross is no longer a necessity in the way forward for human evolution; however, it is still an option. So you see the church felt that they had this power, and it belonged to them. This energy belongs to the earth and we get it by being in contact with it. It is up to us how we use it or if are allowed to use it or not and this is why today the church is losing its power and its people are going back to nature again. The cycle has come around again - "what goes around comes around".

The church is losing its power and this power is going back to the earth. Once again people are coming back to nature and some of the more natural ways of healing such as the practice of meditation and other similar practices.

☯ Rooting and Alignment

We all should have a good rooting to the earth just like the blackthorn. On a physical level this is very important for the skeleton structure of the body. I personally believe that if one is to have a strong and flexible back one must be well rooted to the earth. The earth's energies are sucked up through the feet emanated around the waist and drawn up the centre of the spine, down the arms, and out through the hands in a point called (Laugung) pericardium 8 for healing. There is a constant flow of energy between the earth and the physical, and when this ebb and flow is disrupted in any way the physical body will suffer.

One of the early signs of this is that the back or discs go out of alignment and the person becomes less rooted to the earth. In China it is said, that you can tell a person's age by their posture and the shape of their spine. So lets all become a little more like the blackthorn, which is not all that big physically but its roots go deep down into the earth. I always tell my taiji students in their practice of visualisation, to become like the blackthorn and surround themselves with oak trees. The visualisation of the blackthorn is good for grounding while the oak tree visualisation is good for protection. In this way they are not afraid of nature or its entities but have the greatest respect for it. This will keep everything balanced and in harmony and you may also find that you are in peace and in harmony with everyone and everything around you. You will have a continuous flow of energy from the earth to the physical, keeping you emotionally and spiritually healthy, and in this way; channelling universal energy will come as easy to you as thought, "because the thought is the deed".

☯ What we give out we get back

I'm sure you have often heard the expression, 'come down to earth with a bump'. This is natures' way of looking after us, as we're not here alone.

If for some reason someone gets "too big for their boots" as the saying goes, nature will take care of it. Maybe that person will fall ill or have an accident to shock them back to earth. This is to make them realise that they are going off the path and that this journey is not about material wealth. It also lets us know that what we give out, we get back. This is natures' way of balancing everything out and nature will take care of everything in the fullness of time, no matter how smart we humans think we are, or how powerful we think we have become. Nature is infinitely more powerful and will take care of everything in the fullness of time. This is why it is important to have a good rooting to the earth and to be in harmony with nature and its entities in a non-conditional way. It is very important to respect the nature spirits but not to become their slaves, as everything has a free spirit and everyone is in control of their own destiny.

However, in saying this, our destinies are planned by our higher -selves, i.e. the God within. I believe the old saying 'what's for you won't go by you'. So it is very simple, be good to nature and it in turn, will be good to you. On the other hand, try and mess with nature and this will be the rock you will perish on either in this dimension or the next. We see many examples of this today, where man tries to control nature i.e. the rain forests etc.

☯ Depression and staying rooted

So my spiritual guide says, "do not hold your head up in the clouds - keep your feet firmly on the ground and stay rooted". It is a nice feeling to be up there while meditating but sooner or later, we must come back to earth we must have our passport. We are a physical body in a physical world, touching physical matter etc. This is what happens to people who get depressed. All their esoteric energy gets sucked up through them and they loose their contact with the earth. Sometimes they get so up rooted that they cannot get to grips with anyone or anything. They become so confused and frustrated that eventually some of them take their own lives, as they can see no other way. Their spirits can't help them, because their channels are broken, and because they are not down to earth or grounded. "You must sink before you rise and rise before you sink" meaning; that you must get grounded and find your esoteric roots with the earth and be in harmony with nature. The shaman and all esoteric races knew this; this is why they had so much power. But sadly things changed and man turned on fellow man and slaughtered thousands e.g. the Americans Indians. The second part of this phrase, "rise before you sink", means that you must come to know within yourself that there is much more to you than flesh and bone. Once you see the spirit within the physical, you will become attuned to the spirit of nature. When you reach this realisation you will know that we are all part of the universal system, and that everything must move and work within its laws, in harmony and peace, because everything that is, is total harmony and peace.

☯ The need to be grounded in order to heal

One might imagine from what I have said that we should go around all day talking to oak and blackthorn trees and that healing is achieved by working with the nature spirits and entities. On an energy level this would be true. However, I said that the energy is channelled from the earth up and out through the healer's hands. This energy travels from the cosmic to the earth as energy travels from a greater to a lesser source. When we are in total harmony with the earth and all of its energies we are as close to heaven as to earth and because we are well rooted we can tap into other dimensions. Then we are given power to help others in this dimension through healing.

We do not have to go around all day talking to the trees, if we did this; we would probably be locked up. However, we must remember that mother earth has a place for everything and that the trees, grasses and animals have as much right to be here as us.

Mankind, hopefully, will one day realise that the earth is here to help us, to feed us, clothe us etc. Therefore, if we keep on destroying the earth with our 21st century crap then we are also destroying ourselves. Thankfully there's a great change coming about in that more and more souls are coming here from the spirit world with great gifts. They are being born to re-educate us in saving our planet and to help, bring us back to full spiritual awareness.

So it is not just important to have a good rooting and grounding in order to have a straight back, but it is vitally important to get grounded for the salvation of mankind and our higher -self.

My spiritual guide from the time of 1500 BC says 'He who walks the earth in the bare feet is the blessed one. But he who blocks the earth's energy; is but a fool, and he who cannot find peace and harmony in himself, then no one can save him, and he will surely perish.

CHAPTER 6

Earth Ground Frequencies

LAY LINES AND MERIDIANS (Magnetic Field)

In this chapter I would like to explain things in a more scientific way. We know that everything on this planet is made up of molecules and atoms, each having its own vibration. Even our thoughts have their own vibrations. Everything that you see inside your own home was a thought in someone's mind before it became a reality. The television was always there it only needed someone to invent it. By the use of visualisation and imagination the TV was invented. At first it was a thought vibration on a frequency, and once John Logie Baird tapped into this frequency by his inspiration then the rest was easy. Inspiration works in many ways. As I am writing here there is a vast amount of energy vibrating on different frequencies and I'm picking up on these frequencies by raising the vibrations of my mind to pick up the signals.

One might say then that it is all in the mind, and yes you would be quite right, it is all in the mind. However, the mind is energy, and everlasting and its vibrations are also everlasting. The mind is vibrating at a very fast frequency with a lot of other lay –lines, all vibrating at different frequencies in and around about it. So if we are tuned in enough we can pick up on these frequencies or lay -lines, as they are sometimes called. We can pick up on other energies as well. We can even pick up on the spirit world and other dimensions. That is why the best inspirations come to us in total silence, in our moments of meditation. All of this vast vibrating energy is part of the one universal structure.

I mentioned earlier that one has to lower the vibrations or raise the vibrations to pick up on other frequencies such as the earth lay -lines or low ground frequency wavelength. Try to visualise that you are standing on the moon looking at the earth. The earth will seem a long way away and other stars and planets will surround it. So you could say, from your point of view, that you are standing on the moon and that you are in space. Now as you look at the earth from the moon visualise rings of energy going right around it. Now with the power of your mind come back to earth. You are on the earth planet but you are also in space. This is why I laugh when people do meditation and are always looking up. They are already up. If you find you are looking up, then you are searching for something that is impossible to get out there since you have it within you i.e. within your mind.

The earth is vibrating at a very high frequency. Water diviners, earth dowsers and healers etc have known this for centuries. Many were slaughtered for practising their gift while still more were afraid to mention the subject. It is said that one man or a group of men destroyed all of their knowledge for fear of it getting into the wrong hands. How foolish this was, for this would never be allowed. You cannot work with nature or lay -lines if your intentions are not for the good of others, nor can you do it for personal gain.

☯ Lay- lines & (Magnetic Field)

The earth has ten major lay-lines known to the author, all-vibrating at different frequencies. Seven of them are below the ground and three above the ground. The seven below the ground are known to a lot of people in that field - water-diviners and some scientists. The three above the ground are not very well known apart from some gifted people who work in that field i.e. psychics, mediums, and healers etc.

The lay-lines below the ground are like brooks or rivers. The difference is that those under the ground flow much straighter and faster. They cross over each other at different points on the earth. They cross over one another forming swirling circular pools of energy. These lay lines are not water however but energy moving at an enormous rate, with great vigour and power. They move with such power that it can be hard for us to visualise. Imagine, them like a twister storm and inside this storm, is a point, which springs up through the earth like steam and joins at a universal cosmic point. I said that there were seven of these lay- lines; there could be seventy thousand, as I am just giving the reader a number to work with. The important thing here is that these lay-lines have the same substance or energy vibrations as the meridians system of the physical body.

Usually these lay -lines are more active at particular places on the earth's surface i.e. churches, forts, wells, shrines and healing centres or they are situated in places surrounded by oak trees or ancient circular shrines etc. One of the best examples of this today is the well-known shrine at Stonehenge.

☯ Earth ground frequency wavelengths

There is nothing new about all of this; it has been known for centuries, though scientists however put their own slant to it. Anyone who is sensitive to energy will have no problem tapping into these frequencies, provided they keep an open mind, as the mind is the key to the universe.

The other three lay-lines or earth ground frequency wavelengths are above the ground. Again there could be three thousand of these but I have given the three here, so that no one gets confused. The first one is touching the earth's surface. This is the frequency that comes up through kidney one (k1) the soles of the feet and this is the grounding lay-line.

The second one is vibrating about knee or waist level, depending on a person's height, and the third lay -line is vibrating at waist or chest level. Anyone who has encountered a spirit entity will understand this. The first lay-line is for us humans and the other two are for other entities from other dimensions that are travelling on the astral plane. On the third level one can travel on the astral plane. Yogis and those who levitate usually levitate on the second lay line frequency as it all goes down to vibrations. With total relaxation and breathing skills, one is able to raise their vibrations to second lay -line and break the earth's gravity pull, but I will deal with this later (see levitation).

☯ Raising and lowering our vibrations

We are continually vibrating at a frequency. The fire is vibrating too but at a higher frequency and a stone is vibrating but at a lower frequency. We being human, and having a mind have the power to do both. By the power of the mind we can lower and raise our vibrations and what could be simpler than that. The mind vibrates at a vast wide frequency, which branches out into other frequencies. This is how absent or distance healing is achieved, "believe it and you'll see it, never believe it and you'll never see it ".

So you must have full confidence, trust and control of your own mind for after all it's your mind and it is yours forever. This is achieved by the power of visualisation and imagination. Little children have this power in abundance by keeping the child alive within you the sky is the limit. By having total control of our mind and not letting fear stand in our way all these things are possible.

When children are taught that it is good to daydream they are expanding their mind energy and raising their vibrations. They are linking up with the vast universal energies, which govern everything in all shapes and forms in all dimensions. When we adults have learned to open up our minds in meditation or in similar practice we are on the right path and will find the key to the universe and eternal glory. The Seven Set Practise at the end of this book is one way to learn to open our minds.

☯ Mind Control

Once you make a start then with consistent practice, it will become as easy as brushing your teeth. It is important to achieve control like this over your own mind, not someone else's mind, as this can only lead to a total out of your mind state. With this sort of control over your own mind, life will have a whole new meaning. You will never be bored again. You will be able to travel anywhere in the dimensions or anywhere in the world you want. You will never crave food as you can visualise food and eat it. This is what they do sometimes on arriving in other dimensions. You will be able to wear the same kind of clothes in winter as in summer.

You will keep negativity away; you will be fitter, stay younger and keep your youthfulness a lot longer. You will not get tired as easily and when you do you can recharge the batteries by tapping into the source. You will stay relaxed and happy and you will make others relaxed and happy too. You will never crave for material wealth. You will no longer be afraid of anything, or anyone, therefore you will not worry. You will be able to heal yourself and others, heal the earth, and you will teach others to heal as well. The rule is simple, what you give out you get back, and if you believe you will see but if you never believe you will never see.

☯ Authentic Chi Power

Absent healing or void power or (Ling Kong Jing) is the ability to disrupt the electric magnetic field of an attacker's energy pattern so that the assault can be neutralised and redirected. The aim is to bring about harmony, without physical contact.

Absent Healing or hands off healing is the ability to increase the electric magnetic field of a client's energy pattern, to awaken their body intelligence, neutralise and re -direct blocked energy pathways and patterns. It has the ability to bring about balance, harmony, and well being, without physical contact.

Everything is energy and everything works on vibrations and different frequencies of similar mind state. This is achieved by uniting all of the planes of energies ie physical, mental, emotional and spiritual together with man, Heaven and earth. This is done by disrupting the aura or the dense electric magnetic field of a person's energy pattern in and around their body, neutralising and re - directing the energy for the benefit of that person. So therefore there is no need to have any contact with the physical body what so ever. Absent healing works on vibrations, it works by increasing the electric, magnetic field of a client's energy pattern and by neutralising and re - directing the energy for the benefit of that person's health and well-being. Some healers use a lock of hair so they will pick up on the vibrations on the rest of that client's hair as it is all on the same frequency, but there is no need for this. Some will use mind-to-mind energy, mainly by using the mind of a friend living or passed on to help that person. However, some simply use thoughts. Their thoughts go out into the vast network of the universal energy system and because of their strong vibrations are easily picked up by spiritual guides and are taken care of. "The thought is the deed and if needs be is justified." Spiritual healers work the same way but remember that these are just names. It is all healing and it all comes from the source. In absent healing the thoughts are picked and the energy is linked up to a vast network of spiritual guides, and they will lower their vibrations, and come in esoteric form to do the healing. The healer is only a channel for energy to pass through from a greater source to a lesser source.

However, this does not mean that one should be a passive healer. The healer must take an active part in the healing process, and in this way will have the best results. Some psychics will see these esoteric forms working alongside the healer, passing on messages to the healer in an intuitive way, while they are channelling. This esoteric form is usually a past relative of the client or healer from a higher dimension. Usually they are associated with the healer acting as the healer guide or guides. These guides have to lower their vibrations and the healer or medium will have to raise their vibrations for both of them to communicate on the same frequency. This will usually be done on the third earth ground wave length but not always. Not all healers will be aware of this. Some indeed may not want to be, but they can be certain that they are not doing the healing alone. They also can be sure that everything is at work here from the cosmic to the earth, and if they keep in harmony with everything then the healings will be powerful. They are in control and they decide what channels through them and what does not, and that is why in the history of healing there has never been a case of anyone receiving any harm from a healing. This is another natural law of the universe. The healer has total control during a healing session; however, they have no guarantee or no control over what happens afterwards. I stress this point for healers everywhere; healers should not hold any responsibility, blame or guilt or give any guarantees before or after a healing session. They should however do everything in their power to make life more peaceful and rewarding for their clients. The end result is up to Divine intervention ie the source; as all healing comes from the source and will always be in control, take care and strive to be happy.

CHAPTER 7

Levitation

There are three kinds of levitation known to the author. The first is where you project your mind energy upward away from the dense energy around the earth on the alpha plane. This is the second lay-line above the earth and is where most yogis can levitate to. To do this they sometimes hop around vigorously like a frog above the earth. The physical body in this practice sometimes may hop around or may not. This hopping around is a way of vibrating with the earth's vibrational pulse, this can be achieved by practicing The Seven Set Practice in this book, but this again depends on our spiritual evolution. All of these extraordinary human abilities, as they are called, depend on our spiritual advancements. Some people are known to do this form of levitation in a negative state of mind, in conjunction with meditation only leading to negative results. This form of levitation takes a lot of energy, and you must be in tune with the cosmic forces. You are now acting as a channel between the cosmic and the earth's energies. The earth needs this connection to hold it together. However, this form of levitation, done in a positive state of mind does no harm to the physical, but to bring about this synchronising with the earth is very difficult. This sort of practice I stress once again; all depends on how advanced one is spiritually.

A lot of people may refer to this as an advanced form of meditation, and not call it levitation, but any yogi or guru will tell you that before physical levitation occurs the body will hop around vigorously on the earth. They will also advise you to practice in a crossed leg position i.e. full lotus, to make sure of a safe landing because what goes up must come down.

I call this form levitation and not meditation, because the spirit has levitated away from physical or material reach and is now vibrating on a different level. Such vibrations brought about by this practice, causing the life force meridian to stretch vigorously from the physical body causing it to vibrate and jump around almost uncontrollably.

One of the most fascinating things about this form of levitation is that one would think the heart would be beating faster and that the physical body would be exhausted after this experience, not so. After finishing the physical body will remain calm and relaxed, with no sign of tiredness and the heartbeat will remain normal. This is because the physical has done no work physically; it is just dragged along by the earth's vibrations and the cosmic forces that control the spirit, which is judged on the mind state at the time of practice. Healers and mediums that use this form of levitation to synchronise between the cosmic and the earth and to heal the earth will have very positive results. They will help to balance all the energies of the earth. However, this is an ongoing process and may take another millennium to reach - who knows?

Also all healers are drawn to an earth energy spot i.e. where there is huge link between the cosmic forces and the earth's meridians or lay-lines. Practicing this form of healing in connecting the earth's energies together, keeps it from self-destruction.

☯ Second type of levitation

This type of levitation is a sitting levitation, and is the most wonderful and peaceful of the three types that are mentioned here. It can be used in self-healing or can take place in a self-healing exercise. This is brought about by a deep meditative state while sitting on a chair, usually a good old-fashioned kitchen chair. Through your breathing i.e. reverse breathing (see breathing), and relaxation techniques, you are able to make the physical body very light especially the limbs. You are able to slow down the breathing and heart rate once again as you can in all meditations. But in the first practice your heart rate may increase a little during the period of hopping around, but on finishing the practice it will slow down again almost immediately.

Sit on a chair with both feet flat on the floor. Rest both your arms on the armrests of the chair, practice reverse breathing. You may feel throughout your whole body a sense of lightness as if you were floating in air. This is because your esoteric body has been released from the physical trap, which happened at birth. This is another way of reaching astral travel, but only in a mind state as the physical body stays where it is, sitting on the chair. You may feel so light that your arms will rise upwardly of their own accord. Your spine will be drawn up and straightened and your feet will come off the floor. You may have a great sinking feeling, as sinking into the centre of the earth as often happens in all kinds of meditation and levitation.

Now your esoteric roots are been drawn down into the earth hence the straightening of the spine, so now you can rise spiritually. This is a wonderful feeling of floating upwards and outwards into the vast vacuum of the ever-changing energy of the universe that awaits you.

This is like eating ice cream; you'll never know what it tastes like until you have some. This is one of the safest ways of levitation, but again you must not try to lift your limbs of the chair or floor. This happens almost unaware of your thoughts and happens at a subconscious state.

☯ Third type of levitation

On the third level of levitation which is done standing upright, we break the gravity pull on the physical body away from the earth. Now we vibrate at a much higher frequency by advanced breathing and relaxation skills. Not only will you feel lighter and have a very low heart rate, but also you will actually feel as if you are above the earth. Because you have your eyes closed and you practice privately, you may not have any proof of actually levitating off the earth. In the beginning, the distance is usually only a small gap between your feet and the earth, but as time goes on and with more practice, this gap may get bigger. Some yogis or gurus can levitate some two to three feet of the earth. The best ways to look for proof for yourself is to practice in front of a full-length mirror, and keep your eyes open of course. However, now that you have your eyes open, this will prove more difficult to do as you are waiting for something to happen. As any yogi or guru will tell you, it is difficult enough to meditate with the eyes open not to mention levitate with the eyes open. Another way to look for proof is to practice in the presence of someone you can trust with your secret but be sure it is someone who will not be frightened of what they see.

People may sense different energies or vibrations, or see different things about you. They may see you getting bigger, taller as if you are filling up the whole room. Spiritually you are filling up the whole room, away and beyond with your aura or energy field. As in this realm there is no such thing as an empty space, "within each space is another space". You may think sometimes by putting your hands together and seeing what looks like empty space, that, that is all there is. But there are a lot of different densities in that space and you may discover this by practising "The Seven Set Practice" in this book or doing similar practices.

In this third form of levitation I stress the importance of practising alone, to avoid the ego traps that one is likely to get caught up in. All gifts are special, and should not be used in an egotistical manner, but because of our physical nature it is easy to fall into such traps. Be careful not to fall into an ego trap. Remember that these gifts can be taken away from us in the twinkle of an eye. Like the gift of singing you can lose your gift over night. I am not trying to make the reader feel invincible. No one in this dimension is invincible, no matter how well they practice or how spiritual they become. However, we are very special in the eyes of the universe and the Divine plan of things.

Levitation cannot be taught in the space of these few lines. It acts only as a guide. Anyone studying levitation would be far better off looking for a guide, but this might prove difficult, as most guides will only practice in the comfort of their own privacy. So on a personal note: to practice this in public will make it look like a circus act and it will lose its whole meaning. Who knows, you may look a fool as some mediums sometimes look in front of the camera.

Healing is between the healer and the client, and most importantly between the client and their God, in whatever they perceive their God to be.

Stay within the laws of the universe and one day you will be able to achieve your own potential in whatever that may be. Enjoy your practice and good luck with it.

CHAPTER 8

Cultivating Chi Energy

Cultivating Chi Energy

Chi is the intrinsic energy that sustains all life forms and substances in the universe. It is the life force that regulates the ebb and flow of the vitality of all things. It is referred to as prana in India, shanskrit or rlung in Tibet and ki in Japan. Aristotle referred to it as the soul of energy that exists in all nature where signs of life are to be found. Everything exists in this vast universal energy system i.e. the Alpha and the Omega, with no beginning and no end. This continuous ebb and flow of energy is unfolding and changing and remains as perennial as the grasses. What is now always will be and is moving and evolving at a tremendous rate. We are only scraping the surface of this energy field in modern technology. Everything is evolving, including us humans, at a very fast rate, physically, mentally and spiritually. This is why it is time to learn or should I say, relearn how to cultivate and reroute our internal energy. We can all tap into the earth's energies and there is nothing to be afraid of. The greatest gift that we have as humans is the power of our minds i.e. imagination and visualisation.

☯ Going beyond boundaries

Once you learn to use visualisation and imagination then you have discovered true reality and you have stepped beyond the boundaries of time, space and fear. We are all set on boundaries - saying things like sit down on that chair. We could just as well say sit up on that chair because you are sitting up of the earth onto the high of the chair. So we should not get too stuck on boundaries because in healing there are no boundaries.

When there are no boundaries then there is no fear and if there is no fear then there is no death. When you consider yourself already dead to the illusion of life, there is no fear of dying, because it too becomes an illusion. You are very much alive in spirit and in spiritual values; it is those people that my spiritual guide calls the blessed. He says "there is no death or dying, only transitions of souls from one dimension to the next, and nothing to fear but fear itself". This all goes back to the laws of psychics that energy cannot be destroyed but only transformed, and we and everything in the universe is energy.

We can learn to live forever by cultivating our own internal energy. What you are now you always will be, you are you forever, no matter how long you look at it or how important you become here on this earth. Material things, which were created by the human mind, will pass away and it will make no difference, we create our own reality. This is a journey of life with its ups and its downs and its pluses and minuses. If we do not reach a balance, then we will never reach our higher- self and we will always be searching and going around in circles.

☯ Reincarnation

One can compare reincarnation to the life cycle of a tree. The tree grows up and grows leaves in the springtime. Then in summer it produces beautiful fruit, sheds its leaves in the autumn and dies or looks dead in the winter. Then comes the spring again and new life is given back to the tree, but it's still the same tree, it too is on a journey. Reincarnation is like that; you are still the same being, but wearing a different suit of clothes and acting out your part on this illusionary stage i.e. the earth. However, we have a lazy way with us, and we are always looking for praises or rewards of one kind or another. It's the same when we pass over, we may be too lazy and may not be bothered to reincarnate, Sometimes the higher beings will reincarnate many times, because they have evolved more and are granted greater things, because they did not ask. These greater things are not money or material power but wisdom- this is your reward. That is why a lot of very gifted people here on earth appear to have a lot of wisdom even at a very young age. They may be young physically but are as old as time spiritually. The more wisdom you have the more respect you'll have for everything. Respect is another important part of healing, respect the physical but do not only see the physical; see and honour the spirit that dwells within.

It is up to us if we reincarnate or not as we have all got free will and my guide warns us to be careful how we use this free will. He warns us of greed and of all the confusion, which is the so-called devil of our time. He says we should teach the young meditation and the laws of the universe, and the powers of their own imaginations. He warns me of many things but these have all been written before and some might say that I am copying, so I won't write them here. He says when all of this has passed away; there will be a great peace. It will not be a question of good overcoming evil because there is no such thing as good and evil. When a balance is reached in the minds and hearts of men and women and when they live freely without fear or judgment with no boundaries of religion, race, culture or creed, then there will be total balance and respect for the universal energy. He says, "meditate and stay awake". Mankind is asleep in a rat race of material things but there are a lot of young people born from spirit coming to earth and they will have a great effect on this planet. This evolution has been taking place since the very beginning of earth's existence, but it has speeded up since the 1930s as more evolved souls are coming in greater numbers since the 1950s, and will continue to come till the year 2097 and beyond. He says "these are interesting times to be in the physical because we can all help to make the great change happen, where we will have equality for all, as all men are equal but unique". As he says, "no two snowflakes are the same, but they all look the same, they are still snowflakes, they will transform to water again etc".

I hope this will make your journey a little easier and the road a little shorter. However, it is not written to judge or to dictate to any one group or other. It is written to help people to have an open mind, and to use the power of their mind wisely, so they may find the eternal here and now, because forever is the eternal here and now.

CHAPTER 9

The Seven Set Practice

Each one of these practices opens up one of the seven chakras in the body and works with the seven energies of the planet (sometimes known as the Seven Guardians OF Faith)

All of the practices in this book teach us or relearn to cultivate something that is already within us. How does one teach someone to cultivate something, which they do not see, hear, taste or smell but when given the correct training can feel, or as my students would say get the buzz. At the end of this chapter I have put together some simple postures to help everyone to learn or I should say relearn how to cultivate this vital internal energy. This energy is already within us, and the postures that follow will help you to channel this energy throughout your body. They will also help to increase your energy flow and to gain different abilities and talents, but you must practice. The old masters say that you gain seven different things by doing these practices. Number one, you get fitter and healthier and you are able to keep disease away. Number two, your sexuality increases as you are able to transform your sexual energies and use them for a higher purpose, rather than procreation, meaning as you get older you realise that this energy should be used for greater things. The Chinese and other ethnic races call this regaining the eight bits of life. Number three, you can use it for self healing, healing others and healing the earth. Number four, it can be used for longevity. Number five, you are able to shift disease out of your body and bring harmony between the outer and inner energies. Number six, you are able to be in harmony with the universal energies by drawing more positive people and situations around you. Number seven, you will be able to reach immortality, living in the here and now and being content in that moment of enlightenment.

☯ The Seven Energies of the Universe

The old masters also say that you have seven different energies in the universe. They are cosmic energy, soul energy, spirit energy, mind energy subconscious and conscious energy, chi energy, physical energy and natural or earth energy (electricity or magnetic fields).

These energies make up the universal energy system, and you do seven things to cultivate this energy i.e. hence The Seven Set Practice. So The Seven Set Practice that follows will help you to cultivate and reroute your sexual (or survival) energies and transform them to Zen, spirit or enlightenment. We do seven different things to be able to discharge this energy. Everyone discharges energy, though some people give out more than they have, while others do not discharge enough. Some work all the hours God sends and some do the reverse, there must be moderation in all things to have total balance.

So there are seven things we can do with the energies in our bodies to have the maximum amount of energy at any given time. First we must cleanse it keeping all impure energies away. A lot of people will do this by prayer or meditation while others will use things like fa-jin, explosive body energy leaps similar to sneezing. The North American Indians and the Australian Aborigines use explosive earth leaps. Some yogis will use visualisation and the six healing sounds.

The posture called making the circle, will help you to find harmony with everything above and below. Next you learn to generate your energy. You will learn to draw in the maximum amount of energy at any given time so you are able to draw huge amounts of energy from the earth. Here the posture is called opening the circle. Next you learn to increase this energy and usually this is done through meditation and visualisation. The simple posture for this is called using the circle. As you learn to increase your energy you must learn to circulate it. Now this energy is refined like water and not like treacle. In doing The Seven Set Practice, you will sense if the energy is blocked or stagnant in any part of the body or indeed in someone else's body. So if you get a headache you can shift it by the power of your mind as the mind directs the energy. This can be achieved by mind power i.e. imagination and visualisation, internal viewing and remote viewing. Here the posture is called moving the circle to circulate your energy. Next we learn to store this energy and to have an abundance of it at will because there is an abundance of it about.

We store it in our bone marrow, which is the home of our T cells and immune system, keeping us strong and healthy with a very strong bone structure, known in some martial arts as tiger bones. Here the posture is called holding the circle. Next we learn to preserve our energy so we are able to withstand different climatic conditions like great heat, cold, wind, damp etc, which affect all the organs in our bodies e.g. the kidney's do not like the cold and the spleen does not like the damp etc. By preserving our energy, we are able to eat less food and sleep less and yet have a better quality of sleep and rest. Sometimes through the action of dreams and nightmares we use up a lot of energy. So the next posture is to preserve energy ie becoming the circle. To preserve energy simply means to use less energy for any task, and once you learn to preserve this energy you must learn to discharge it openly and willingly. As a universal law, universal energy must be allowed to flow in and out in total harmony and balance; example of this, is money; health; and wealth. You can now discharge this energy to others in the form of healing yourself, healing others, teaching others to heal, and eventually healing the earth, which is what this book is all about, this is achieved by practicing the last posture, called releasing the circle.

☯ The Seven Set Practice

I've put together seven postures to help you to cultivate your own internal powers. It is very important to get rooted to the earth so we will always start with the feeling of being stuck to the earth. So you must sink before you rise and rise before you sink (i.e. making the circle)

By practising The Seven Set Practice you will be able to cultivate your own internal energy and learn to discharge universal energy through you as a healer. However, you must practice. These postures are only physical things to do to help you get there; the end result is the mind state. Remember the thought is the deed.

So for those of you who would have very little visualisation skills I have also given you physical postures to practice to help you reach the same results, that is to discharge the energy.

However, in saying this there is nothing physical you can do, or learn to do, to discharge this energy. In order to discharge this energy, you must do nothing. This may sound ridiculous, but as I said earlier, you as the healers are not doing anything, so there is nothing to do only be there. However, you must take an active part with your mind in the healing and not be a passive healer. However, if you try too hard or think too much you will block the ebb and flow of this universal energy and will have little or no success.

The only thing you have to do is simply be there, and have confidence in your abilities as a healer and to have confidence in your gifts and guides etc, it is as simple as that. You might ask if it's as simple as that, why can't everyone reach this state. Well this is because we have become too materialistic and too attached to the physical and because of this are afraid to let go. Once people are able to let go they become just energy evolving and revolving with the same ebb and flow as the universe. In letting go they become a minuet part of this universal energy.

Everything that has ebb and flow is a minuet part of us all.

So to give you the best of both dimensions, there are fourteen postures instead of seven. The first seven act on the physical plane. The next seven act on the esoteric plane by the use of imagination and visualisation. So you are now given a choice of physical or esoteric training, the choice is yours. However, in saying that you might have to practice first with the physical postures. Whichever of these postures you choose you can be sure that they will help you to have a better quality of life and to live a much fuller life, as life is for living. The ultimate aim of anyone is to be relaxed and to be happy in whatever way they perceive that to be, and once you are relaxed and happy you make others relaxed and happy. You will also have good control over your health. In other words, when something goes wrong you can fix it. "Remember the thought is the deed" So now we know that each posture has two parts i.e. esoteric and physical and to keep things simple I have named them *THE SEVEN SET PRACTICE.*

We do these postures to harness, cultivate and discharge universal energy. I no longer call it chi energy since we are not trying to cultivate internal energy as that is already there and any way we don't want to deplete our own energy. We are not even trying to cultivate universal energy but we are in fact letting our conscious know that we are one with this mass of cosmic force.

☯ The Importance of breathing correctly

Usually when I am giving a workshop on cultivating energy, I will ask a few of the members to take a deep breath. Sadly, most of them if not all of them, breathe high up in the chest and are only using two thirds of their lung capacity. If they are smokers, then they are only using one third of their lung capacity. We should all breathe lower down in the lower abdominal region of the diaphragm lowering and lifting naturally while using all of our lungs capacity. As children and later as adults we tend to tense up and stop breathing naturally and we start breathing high up into the chest. However, when in a subconscious state, we will automatically start breathing down in the lower region again. By the time we reach middle age we will have become very shallow breathers and will now be breathing high up in the chest all the time. This is due to our life styles and lack of practice in breathing correctly while in the conscious state. Everything that we do in the conscious state will be carried through to the subconscious and everything that we know in the subconscious state can be tapped into at a conscious level. So you may have to practice natural breathing now for some time before you get it right, but after awhile it will become second nature and there will be no need to practice. It is a bit like riding a bike, you might fall off a few times but with practice you will be able to ride that bike with no hands so to speak. In natural breathing you will be breathing a lot slower and deeper and down into your abdominal region. You will be using your full lungs capacity and any doctor will tell that the more oxygen you have in your lungs the better off you will be. You will have more energy, stay fitter, and be much healthier.

There are two kinds of breathing. They are post natal or natural breathing and pre natal or reverse breathing. I never teach breathing skills in my workshops, I just tell them to watch a young child as it breathes. On the in breath its belly will raise and go out and on the out breath its belly will sink or go in. I always tell my students to smile inwardly when practising their breathing skills in taiji etc.

☯ The Uniqueness of the Seven set practice

Now although these are similar to other forms of meditation, Celtic or Tibetan etc., they are in fact unique, because this is the first time they have been written or taught.

They are, as I said, a part of my own imagination and wisdom, brought to me through my spiritual guide, they are a one off. Now I am not saying, that throughout history people did not know or practice things like cleansing or increasing and discharging energy but that nothing like this has ever been presented in this order i.e. physically and metaphysical before. That is why I think that these practices will make healing and working with energy an ordinary every day occurrence in the 21st century in all walks of life. The circle I refer to in The Seven Set Practice is the circle of life or the tree of life, which is universal energy. In "The Seven Set Practice" there are two parts in every posture just as in nature you have two of anything to give total balance. So each posture has a yin and a yang, positive and negative qualities in order to achieve total balance.

☯ Points before Practising

There is no special time to practice but it is best in the early morning or at dawn. There are no hard and fast rules except it is best not to practice before going to bed. Make sure that your clothes are loose and comfortable. It is best to practice without a break as this will help to discipline you and give you a sense of commitment. However, if you break the cycle don't worry as you can always start again. Don't take the practice too seriously or too lightly, just allow a happy medium and follow the instructions here as best you can. Have fun with your practice and let them become as much a part of you as you are part of the universal energy.

Remove your shoes and yes you can do your practice indoors. I always find it better to practice these postures in doors where the energy is more concentrated, not like the taiji where I find it better to practice outside. Your breathing is natural like a small baby, and there is no need to count the breath, as this will only distract you.

It's best to practice in a quiet place at first, but after a while it will not matter where you practice. After practising for the first 21 days, rest for the next 3 days. Do not repeat these exercises more than two or three times a day, as they are very potent. Never practice if you feel a bit under the weather, rest and let the body heal naturally, in this way your sickness should only last two to three days. However, if you listen to what your body, mind and spirit are saying and look for the signs, you will not be sick too often, colds and flu's should be at a minimum. Remove things like rings, watches and money as they can also distract you.

All these postures are practised standing up. So make sure to have your hips straight and your gravity in the centre.

Keep your tongue on your upper pallet.

Keep your eyes half closed to help you concentrate.

Do not eat anything for fifteen minutes before and after practice.

Before practising allow a few minutes of stillness standing quietly and finding your centre as these postures are not just your ordinary run of the mill type of training. On the esoteric level they go much deeper. Remember you are tapping into the vast cosmic forces and everything in it. You are now working at an energy level and since energy has no consciousness, it will travel anywhere at will. So this is why you must protect yourselves, this is important to achieve the end results.

Some of the things we do in these postures are similar to the ancient traditions of generating or drawing energy from the earth. The energy as we know is drawn from the earth up through the soles of our feet through the acupuncture point in Chinese medicine known as kidney one (K1). This is done sometimes by uncontrollable body energy explosive leaps, known in taiji, as fa-jin leaps. I refer to this sort of thing to my students as the shakes. Dragging your feet on the earth will cause you to vibrate with the earth. This will not usually happen right away but after some weeks or months of practice you will vibrate. This is a cleansing process getting rid of all the toxins and negative energies in the body, there, s nothing to worry about.

As the energy travels from the cosmic to the earth, we are able to pick up the frequency or vibrations with our feet, which act as huge conductors. The feet are very sensitive and this sensitivity is reflected in the fingers, wrists and palms of the hands acupuncture point (Laugung) or pericardium 8.

We drag our feet in a counter clockwise direction to stimulate the earth ground frequency wavelength. In the fourteenth century lots of women were branded as witches in England and in other parts of Europe and were burned for their beliefs and practices. The same can be said of the American Red Indians and other pagan cultures. They were slaughtered in their thousands because of their dance and of their contact with the earth or earth spirits. Anything that has an energy system has a spirit, which appears as an aura or magnetic field. Gladly to the present day there are some cultures that walk around in the bare feet and are close to the earth. Sadly there are those who have little or no regard for the earth and continue to destroy the true nature of the spirit within, the destruction of the rain forests is an example of this. This can only lead to man's destruction. For once we as man mess with nature and show disrespect and disregard for the universal energy, then man can only perish.

So in other words in order for one to be healed or develop the gift of healing we must be in contact with the earth and dance to its vibrations.

Within the mind comes the dance.
Within the dance there is stillness.
Within the stillness there is power, and from that power comes peace

☯ Cleansing Breath

After standing in a relax stance for a few minutes, now draw your hands up and out from your body palms facing up to about shoulder height. Take a deep breaths filling up the lungs to capacity and holding the breath for a little. Now drop your hands down, palms facing forward, down and out at the sides. Next lean forward from the waist and let the breath go out of the lungs in a huge flow while producing a sound something like the sound of the word ha -h-a haa. It is important that you let the breath go out naturally, to the point that you cannot get any more air out of your lungs still in the bent over position. Pushing your hand forward will help you visualise the stale air leaving your lungs. This will also help you to let go in future practices. As you stand up bring your hands to starting position again and relax and start the cleansing process again. Do this practice three times before any of The Seven Set Practices as this is not only gets stale air out of the lungs but also helps to break down and get rid of any toxins in the body, and because of this it is an excellence body builder. Now we are ready to start The Seven Set Practice.

ENERGIES OF THE PLANET

The seven energy centres in the body related to the seven energies that have come into the planet.

The first energy is to with will, power and action and vibrates to the colour of red

The second energy, which is deep blue, which is helping our planet to evolve now, is to do with love and wisdom.

The third energy is green and is to with, using your mental process to get the will of God grounded on earth.

The fourth energy is yellow and is to do with the arts, music, dance, literature, film etc it is still with us, but it came in very strong in the turn of the last centaury as the world had very dark vibrations.

The fifth energy, which is orange, is to do with the new age, which has got much stronger since the new millennium. Teaching us to use our mental powers and bring forth new skills and scientific development.

The six energy is the Christ like energy which is indigo it came in 2000 years ago embodied in Christ. It stands for religion idealism and devotion. It is now moving away as it is no longer needed. This time there is more emphasis on the seven rays to do with purification and self-empowerment and oneness with spirit.

The seventh energy is to with the purple ray of purification and healing and it is most active on the planet as we speak.

There is an eight energy, it is white, which is a deep cleansing energy, we are now getting a chance of coming out of the dark and heavy vibrations of the past and moving into light vibrations with total balance of Yin and Yang.

☯ No 1a Making the circle.

Do this practice three times. This exercise cleanses the physical

Start off this posture in the same way as the last breathing posture, standing still rooted and relaxed.

Now draw both hands up in a circular fashion, palms facing outwards, circling your right hand in a clockwise direction and circle your left hand in an anti -clockwise direction keeping your hands in front of your chest about a face distance apart. Do this nine times. This will unite the outer forces with the inner forces, the above and below and so bring balance and harmony within your space.

If, however you want to use bright lights or colours, use a mantra or pray or do anything of your choice this is entirely up to you as there are no hard or fast rules in these practices. Now join the thumb of your right hand to the index finger of your right hand and do the same with the left hand, holding your left hand down below the navel, palm turned up and looking at you and holding your right hand up, palm turned down looking away from you. Next bring your right hand up and start tapping a point, between your eyes lightly with the joint fingers, as if knocking on a door. Continue this vibrating or taping for some 3 to 5 minutes. At the same time bend your knees slightly downward and inward, sinking all of your weight down. You can use visualisation for this so with the power of your mind, you can extend your energy field, three feet down into the centre of the earth. This may sound somewhat difficult to beginners, but with practice it is amazing the control one gets over the mind in a very short time of practice.

Your feet will now be used as conductors, magnifying the powerful frequency of the earth energies below causing it to be sucked up through your feet at kidney one (k1) and vibrating through your whole body because of the magnetic ions (an electrical charge atoms or group of atoms) in your energy field. This will magnify the energy now to such an extent that your whole body may vibrate mildly or sometimes vigorously depending on how long you have been practising, or depending on how much toxins you have built up, and how much cleansing has to be done.

Now on the last part of this physical practice, open out your hands and relax them further by letting them hang down loosely on either side of your body. Extend your fingers with a little tension. After some weeks of practising your whole body may vibrate and indeed could leap forward uncontrollably. Your whole body may be off the ground for a split second during these leaps, this is known in taiji martial arts practice world as fa-jin, explosive energy. I call it an expression of power and the magnifying of energy between the earth and the physical. This is somewhat like sneezing, your eyes will half close, and your whole body will vibrate or leap forward. This all happens involuntarily as there is no message working on a conscious state. It just happens and you must let it happen. Never try to leap forward, this will block the ebb and flow straight away. Now these leaps may go on for quite some time, but after months of practice everything will settle down and you will have great enjoyment from it. This is why it is better to practice alone, or with someone who understands you. Otherwise they might think that you are losing it. You can be sure that this is a natural way of making contact with the earth and the nature spirits. It is also a sure way of getting rid of any toxins, past negative patterns or blockages in your energy field and so helps you become a healer. In order to heal you must clean up your own space or energy field first.

☯ No 1b Making the circle

Do this practice three times
Esoteric level

Now the second part of this practice is on the esoteric level. Through use of the power of your mind, imagination and visualisation, we take an energy shower.

Stand in the same relaxed position, feet shoulder width apart, hands down by your sides, relax and breathe naturally. Next raise both your hands up slowly over the top of your head, palms facing up. Now with the power of your mind visualise cosmos energy coming in through your hands at a high frequency, feeling your hands getting warm and tingly. Now stretch out your fingers, keeping them relaxed, this will bring a lot more energy into the hands. Now when you think you have a good supply of energy turn your palms over i.e. facing down over the top of your head, and visualise the energy coming down through your whole body healing anything that may be wrong with it, (whether physical, mental or emotional,) as it passes. Visualise the energy passing through your whole body, and absorbing it like a sponge would absorb water, healing anything in its path. As energy will travel from a greater to a lesser source, if you have trouble with your throat just stop there for a few minutes and fill the throat Chakra with loving blue healing energy, as blue is the colour for healing. Then you can move on down to your heart and once again, by the power of your mind, you can visualise the very structure of your heart or internal organs. With practice you might be able to see your client's blockages as well. However, don't worry if you can't see anything, as your subconscious knows this already.

Now continue visualising this energy passing down and out through the soles of your feet at kidney one (KI). With the power of your mind visualise it going down and away three feet below you. This is the extended energy field and with more practice and using mind projection, you will be able to send your energy much further. This is a very useful practice, as you will develop a much stronger energy field (see absent healing).

☯ Health Benefits of making the circle

(Opens up the Third Eye Chakra, which is responsible for Intuition Clairvoyance, Imagination and Perception). This will open up your psychic and your third eye Chakra, and there will be a great sense of peace flowing through you, which may come as messages from your guide or guides etc. It is associated with the pineal gland and controls the left eye, lower brain, nose, ears and the endocrine system. This Chakra vibrates to the colour of indigo, or light purple the colour unity and wisdom.

If you practice both of the above postures, you will be strengthening and invigorating your whole self, and you will become very sensitive to the forces around you. You will develop high intuition, wisdom and knowledge. You will start to look at life from a different angle and be more appreciative of your own life and the lives of others, plants and animals etc. You will realise that everything has a purpose and in order to have good health you must be in harmony with everyone and every thing around you.

☯ No 2a Opening the circle

Physical level
Do this practice three times.

The earth spin is clockwise in direction if you are living in the Northern Hemisphere and the earth spin is anti clockwise direction if you are living in the Southern Hemisphere. Just look at the water going down your sink, note this important point for this practice.

Standing again in the starting position, stay nice and relaxed with hands loosely by your sides. We are ready to begin the next practice to generate energy. Bring up your hands slowly, palms to navel level, palms facing down. Hold them there for a short time and breathe naturally. Now sink your weight or mind down to the feet making your body much heavier as if you were stuck to the earth. Next simply try to walk forward in a counter clockwise direction in accordance with earth spins. So if you're living in the Northern Hemisphere you will turn anti clockwise, and start dragging your feet on the earth below you. This will activate the first lay line on the earth surface as your feet are being used as huge conductors to magnify this frequency. You can use your hands to help with the walking or dragging as if climbing up a steep hill. You will feel very heavy and stuck to the earth. Use the power of your mind to visualise energy coming up through your body and into your hands. After some months of practice your hands may feel hot and sweaty, tingly, numb or slightly painful. They may appear blotchy with white and red spots or have a red spot in the centre of them. But just let all of this happen naturally as you will generate a lot of energy in this practice. So do not do this practice if you want to go to sleep. Practice this in the morning if possible or if you feel a bit tired, again practice alone.

☯ No 2 b Opening the circle

Esoteric level
Do this practice three times

In the normal relaxed, standing position, simply cup both your hands and imagine a ball of energy or fluff in your hands. Now just move it from left to right, like you would do if you had a real ball in your hands and as you move it imagine it getting bigger, at the same time shift your weight from left to right.

Next bring both your hands up to your temple and place the first two fingers lightly on the temple. Turn in a counter clockwise direction three times in accordance with earth spins. So if you're living in the Northern Hemisphere you will turn anti clockwise.

. This will open up your base Chakra and there will be a great sense of power flowing through you. Now when you feel a lot of energy between your hands just place them on your navel, which is your home base and the safest place to be. You will start to feel very secure and confident in yourself. When everything settles down bring both your hands outwards and away from the body, up and around and down past your centre, with the thumbs and the first two fingers touching briefly at your waist level. Then separating at your navel slowly and out and down to the sides in an out breath. Every upward or inward movement is done with an in breath and every outward and downward movement is done with an out breath.

☯ Health Benefits of opening the circle.

Opens the base Chakra that helps with smell, individuality, security, health and courage.

This practice is extremely good for keeping you grounded and healthy and opening up the doors of your mind to become a healer. This practice will give you great energy if you are tired. It is associated with the adrenal gland and controls the skeleton, nervous system, sense of smell, strong and flexible spine, bones, teeth, and nails. It is associated with stability, stillness grounding and courage. This Chakra vibrates to the colour of red, the colour of passion and vitality.

☯ No 3 a Using the circle

Physical level
Do three times

Stand once again with your hands down by your sides and bend your knees to lower your centre of gravity. Take a step forward with your right foot, with the ball of the foot touching the floor. Next with both hands held out in front of you, palms facing down, circle them around in a clockwise direction as if you were stirring a big pot of water. However, in this case your mind is stirring a huge pot of energy. Turn the palms to the right nine times. Now repeat the same on the opposite side. This time with the left foot touching the floor, hands held over the knees palms facing down, stir this time in an anti clockwise direction six times to the left - do this practice three times.

☯ No 3 b Using the circle

Esoteric level
Do this practice three times

On this level we simply bring both hands up and join them as if in prayer and then rest them on the top of your head. Now with the power of your mind visualise cosmic energy hitting your hands, your fingers acting like antenna, increasing the energy flow coming up through your feet and down through your head. Visualise this energy going right through your whole body to a point below the navel and mixing your prenatal energy with your postnatal energy. Any energy below the waist is prenatal and any energy above the waist is postnatal. Next separate your hands and bring them down in front of your chest, arms bent slightly with extended fingers, with a little physical tension. This will bring a lot more energy into the hands, causing the eyes to flare up, and become fiery like a wild animal, stimulating the reptilian brain. This practice will test your visualisation and imagination skills. However, after a while you will be able to sense the two energies mixing up in and around your navel or your home base, increasing your energy potential, so you will have more of energy to go around.

Now at this stage of the practice you have really opened the floodgates of the forces around you so before moving on to the next practice rest for three days.

☯ Health Benefits of using the circle.

Opens up the Throat Chakra and therefore aids hearing, communication, kindness, truth and loyalty. It is associated with thyroid gland and controls the lymphatic system the metabolism, hands, arms, shoulders, mouth, vocal cords, lungs bronchial system, sense of sound the throat, neck and voice. It is associated with self-expression confidence and truth. This Chakra vibrates to the colour of blue, the colour of communication and healing.

This practice will again increase your energy flow while breaking down any barriers or blockages in your body and any blockages in the flow of energy from the earth to the physical, so you may shake a little.

☯ No 4 a Moving the circle

Physical level. Circulating energy
Do this three times

In this practise it is essential to have a loose waist. When the energy comes up through the feet via the knee joint, it circulates around the waist, goes up the govern vessel or back, down through the arms and out through the palms at (Laugung) or pericardium 8. In order to get a loose waist, we must make the distinction between the upper and lower body. So instead of the hips moving, we must have the waist moving. In other words, everything must be moving from below as in taiji practise. One way to achieve this is to sit on a stool, feet flat on the floor and stretch both your arms out to the side, and swivel from left to right. In this way the hips will not move it will only be the waist. Continue this exercise until you find your waist getting much looser and stronger, so the muscles around your waist become familiar to you again. You will notice this strengthening of the muscles around the waist when lifting heavy objects, as they would normally feel much heavier. This is because you are now using the whole band of muscles around your waist, the adducted muscles, rather than using your triceps and biceps or possibly a straight back.

So now when you have a nice loose waist and a good strong back you are ready to begin the next practice, which is moving the circle.

Now start off once again from the usual relaxed position. Just simply turn your waist to your left and at the same time bring both your hands up, left palm facing down and right palm facing up. Now as you turn to the left, bring your right palm over and across the top of your left wrist. Now as you turn back again to the right, bring your left palm up through your centre palm facing up, and over your right wrist. Continue in this fashion with right palm over left wrist and left palm over right wrist while making sure that your waist is still nice and relaxed and loose. Now continue moving in a circular fashion at the waist and at the same time turning your arms up as if they were growing up out of the ground. This action happens involuntarily, as the twisting of both your feet into the ground in a toe and heel fashion brings it about. This action stimulates and circulates the energy through your whole body. You literally are to some extent growing out of the ground with some tremendous twists in your waist to strengthen your whole body. The foot work here gives the correct balance. In other words, you only draw and circulate as much energy as required to over come any blockages. This is a hard practice, so take it easy at first, but it is a wonderful natural way of building yourself up, rather than pumping iron as man and machine - no contest. When the twisting has stopped, triggered by your subconscious, as this is an involuntary action, we finish by bringing both hands down and back to the centre. Rest before starting the esoteric side of this practice.

☯ NO 4 b Moving the circle

Esoteric level
Do this practice three times

Imagine a big pot of energy in your centre at navel level or your home base. Now with the breath and the power of your mind, breathe on the fire in your navel and the energy will change state and rise. In the same way you put more heat on the fire to boil a kettle, the water in the kettle will change state and rise. Place your hands with thumbs first finger and middle finger together and hold them there in a triangle shape over your navel at a 45-degree angle thumbs pointing in towards your navel. Hold them there until you get a nice sensation of heat and tingling.

Next allow your hands to slowly move up the front of your body to solar plexus level. This time thumbs face your solar plexus but not touching. Again hold them there for some time approx. 5 to 10 minutes and visualise nice energy around this space.

Now move your hands up to the middle of your forehead or third eye, this time with thumbs pointing down and fingers pointing up. Hold them there until you get some kind of sensation between your eyes, perhaps a tingling or bright lights or colours etc. Now bring your hands up and over the top of your head, thumbs resting on the top of your head and hold them there while imagining energy circulating in and around your whole body. When you have finished bring your hands down through your centre and out by your sides.

☯ Health Benefits of moving the circle

Opens up the Solar Plexus Chakra and assisting sight, energy, radiance, power and self-control. It is associated with the pancreas and controls the sense of sight, the autonomic nervous system, lower back, muscles, liver spleen, stomach, gall bladder and the digestive system. It is also associated with self-control, vitality and inner strength. This Chakra vibrates to the colour of yellow, the colour of power and inner strength

You have now learned to stimulate the energies in your energy field or in your Chakras and meridians so you can now circulate energy anywhere in your body. If your energy gets blocked and you develop a backache or headache you can move it at will by the power of your mind and in this way keep healthier. This practice is great for your digestive system, breaking down toxins and getting rid of stagnant energy in your energy system.

☯ No 5 a Holding the circle

Physical level Storing energy
Practice three times

Start from a relaxed standing position. Now bring both your hands up to your centre as in prayer, breathing in as you come up. Next push both joined hands out in front and away from the body while breathing out. Now take them back in again while breathing in. Next push both hands down towards your middle fingers pointing down and breathe out. Now draw them back up on an in breath and push them outwards once more, this time breathing out. Now on an in breath take them back to the centre and on another out breath push both your hands upwards, pushing them up through your centre in line with your nose, about three inches above your head. Now on the final out breath, drop your hands down separating them in the centre.

93

☯ No 5 b Holding the circle

Esoteric level
Do this practice three times

Now from the starting standing position, bring both hands up and cross them at the wrists at navel level, right over left for males and left over right for females. At the same time sink your weight or concentration down and bend your knees downwards and inwards. This will again cause some shaking brought about the magnifying of your ions in your meridian system and energy field with the earth's magic pulse. Now the earth and the physical body act as polar opposites. This is a very powerful practice as you are now tapping into the second lay line above the earth, the lay-line that yogis usually levitate on

Stand there until the shaking has stopped and everything settles down. Now separate your hands and bring them back down to your sides and relax before moving on to the next practice.

☯ Health Benefits of holding the circle

Opens up the navel Chakra and aids taste, emotions, desire, pleasure and change.
It is associated with the gonadal glands sexual organs and control the sense of taste, the reproductive organs, kidneys, bladder feet and legs. It is also associated with enthusiasm, creativity, relationships, fear and anger. This Chakra vibrates to the colour of orange, the colour of creativity and desire.

Now you can store this energy and pack it into the T cells of the bone marrow for a strong immune system, giving you healthier and stronger bones known as tiger bones in some cultures. You can hold more energy in your navel for further use and therefore become stronger and much healthier. You learn to preserve your energy and to have more of it to go around for healing etc.

☯ No 6 a Becoming the circle

Physical level
Do this practice three times

Now once again from the usual relaxed standing position bring both hands up to chest height, arms bent and palms facing down. Again with the power of your imagination, which should be coming along fine by now imagine your roots going right down through the earth and raising your spirit or esoteric self upwards. This will tap you into the third lay line of the earth's frequency and is what yogis do to break the earth gravity. Now from there out stretch your arms to both sides, left palm facing up and right palm facing down. This practice like the others is best done in the early morning. Standing there with outstretched arms; now turn your body three times in a clockwise direction if living in the Northern Hemisphere and turn anti clockwise if living in the Southern Hemisphere. Now after standing there nice and relaxed you will feel very tall. The reason for this is that your spirit has grown and it is now stronger. This practice will open up your higher intuition and the doors to your subconscious and beyond, opening your awareness to spirit. After a while when all the messages are released to your subconscious, it will be time to come back to earth and once again use the simple technique shown earlier.

You realised now that there is much more to you than just the physical shell. By now you will have found your higher self and your purpose on this planet. However, this is your universal secret and no one else's. You may find that after this practice you may even be walking around, somewhat up in the clouds for a few days.

Keep doing the grounding technique of coming back to centre and down to earth and everything will be fine.

☯ No 6 b Becoming the circle

Esoteric level. Preserving energy
Do this practice three times

Now after many months of practising the whole seven set there will not be a lot of difference in the physical or esoteric side of this particular practice or indeed any of the practices. It all depends on one's imagination and visualisation skills.

Now once again stand in a relaxed position with hands down by your sides, feet shoulder width apart and breathing naturally and relaxed. Now bring both hands up and out from your sides slowly like a big bird wings. At the same time with the power of your mind visualise your esoteric roots going away down deep into the centre of the earth and feel the sensation of your spirit or esoteric self rising and floating upwards. Continue moving your arms upwards and outwards. Now when they reach shoulder height turn your palms upwards with your eyes in a fixed gaze and relax. If you wish you can close your eyes in this practice to help your concentration and visualisation. Now all of this is done on the one breath. Now out stretch your fingers and just stay there in total silence. You will not even hear yourself breathing and indeed after some time of practising, anyone watching you may think that you are not breathing at all. This is because you are now in a total subconscious state or trance, known in some religions as slain in spirit and this can take some time to reach. However, with practice you can reach this state just by thought. This is a very powerful practice and will open up many doors in the subconscious. In other words, this is your passport from your conscious to your subconscious, and this makes it a very useful practice before under going any healing. This will turn your own energy to Zen and raise the spirit and vibrations to the third lay line above the earth. So now you can cross from one dimension to another, from the conscious to the subconscious in the twinkle of an eye. This will help with attunement, so that other higher entities can lower their vibrations and so that the two energies become one. This is your passport to becoming a healer. This is a very old practice and it is still used in some ethnic cultures; a wonderful practice indeed. Although it is a lovely feeling up there in your mind one must come back to earth. This is achieved again simply by bringing your hands in towards each other, fingers touching, and palms pointing down. Now on an out breath bring them slowly through your centre, separating them at your navel and relaxing them down by your sides. If you try and get back to earth so to speak or come out of meditation without this simple technique you will literally come down to earth with a bump. You will think that you have fallen of a few steps. This sort of experience happens to people when they are dropping off to sleep. In sleep our spirit or esoteric body travels on the astral plane but sometimes through fear it gets shot back into the physical body. This is why we can sometimes feel worse after a night's sleep than we should do. This is because we have not got our passport or don't know how to use it (see astral travel)

☯ Health Benefits of Becoming the circle.

Opens the Crown Chakra i. e. Infinite, Oneness with the infinite & Divine Wisdom.

It is associated with the pituitary gland and controls the right eye, upper brain, central nervous system and unity with the divine universal consciousness. This Chakra vibrates to the colour of white, the colour of purity and light.

You learn to keep your energy fresh and free flowing. Negativity will flow through you without affecting you. Changes in climatic conditions will not affect you. You will be able to wear the same clothes in winter as in summer and you will not need a fan in summer. You will gain in overall health, increase in energy and efficiency and decrease in sleep requirements. While sleep quality is increased, hunger and food intake diminishes and the capacity to handle stress increases. You may feel an improvement in your peace of mind, your relationships with others, self-confidence, self -esteem, success and quality of life. You are able to stay in the centre and be at one with the universal forces. You learn to take care of your own energy and to preserve it and not let it leak out or drain away. You learn to draw energy from outside. You begin to live better, eat and sleep better, choose supportive friends and situations. Learn to take in bigger charges of energy, have more control of your emotions and finally become more virtuous and good.

☯ No 7a Releasing the circle

Physical level. Discharging the energy
Do this practice three times

On the physical level this practice is quite powerful looking, but you know yourself that everything is in the centre and in control. However, on the esoteric level it is the complete opposite, no flaring of the eyes no jumping around, none of that. You will look totally relaxed, not a worry in the whole wide world. You will be full of compassion and this may show in your eyes, as the eyes are the mirrors to the soul or other dimensions. You may look as if you are in prayer but not uttering a single word, everything now is working with you and for you for the benefit of all in all dimensions. To Start, you simply start moving the weight of your feet from left to right while circling the waist at the same time, simply cup both your hands and imagine a ball of energy or fluff in your hands. Now just move it from left to right, like you would do if you had a real ball in your hands and as you move it imagine it getting bigger, as you did in the second practice opening the circle 2b. Extend your roots right down into the centre of the earth if they are not already down. Now circle both hands way out in front of the body about chest height and continue them round to they meet in the centre palms facing up. Now in this position push your palms slowly outwards in front of your face as if holding up a large ball of energy. Next bring them back down through your centre, and circle them the opposite way, palms are facing down. Again on an out breath push your palms upwards and out to face height, the same as before. Now from there, circle your palms in the same way as you did in the first practice, i.e. bringing your palms around and up through your centre. Palms gradually coming together and touching the backs of each other, as they turn and fold up out over your head, and extend the fingers outwards and downwards bringing all of your emotions to the surface before relaxing them down by your sides to finish the practice, do this practice three times.

However, you may not stay still here as this sort of movement can again cause the body to leap forward in an explosive manner causing the eyes to flare up. This sort of explosive energy can be seen in some of the internal martial arts. This is because the spirit and the body and the earth are at one. This practice is given here to help you strengthen your meridians to cope with the extra flow of energy your body is now receiving. This is also a good way of keeping the earth's energy together. All ethnic races know this and this is why they do so much jumping around on the earth.

The body may vibrate here again or indeed could start jumping and leaping so vigorously that after a while one might think that they would be out of breath and extremely tired but not so. These vibrations are natural and go with the natural flow of the earth's vibrations; in fact, it will be the complete opposite. Once this experience is over it is time to relax and release the energy we now have created. This is done by imaginatively drawing a figure eight with your right hand held in front of you palm facing up as if you were drawing a figure eight on a blackboard. We imaginatively draw the figure eight three times and at the end of the movement we fan out our right hand, something similar to a champion dart player seen in slow motion. As the dart is release the hand fans out soft and relaxed to guide the dart to it target. In the same way in this practice we fan out the hand, fingers soft and relax, to release the energy and to guide it to whatever intention we see fit, (by the power of the mind of course).

When releasing the energy, we may experience a slight quivering of the hand but that natural and a good sign that you have made progress so yes this is good. You will feel like a new person, full of energy, totally in control, no fear, and you will have reached the stage of total peace or enlightenment, felling calm, relaxed and ready for the final practice.

☯ No 7 b Releasing the circle

Esoteric level. Discharging energy
Do this practice one time only.

From a standing position take a small step forward with your right foot and bring your left hand up to your heart Chakra or centre. Next bring your right hand up to shoulder level right side, as if you were going to stop someone and ask him or her a question. Hold the thumb, index and middle fingers up but relaxed, and fold the other fingers down slightly, but not closed fully or tense. This is a well-known symbol in many cultures and religions through the world, and there are many reasons for this. When the hands are held open like this it is the maximum point of energy discharge from the physical. The left hand is the receiving hand and is pointed towards the heart, without the compassion of the heart there can be no healing. It is a symbol of truth; the right hand is the giver and the symbol of peace.

These are the symbols of truth, love and compassion and they emphasise the main energy point on the hands. By holding your hands in this way and having your heart in the right place you will achieve the full flow of energy from the cosmos to the earth and from the earth to the physical. This symbol can be seen all over the world and is a symbol of truth and has nothing at all to do with religion. To me it is a symbol of peace and man finding his or her higher -self. After doing this practice there is the feeling of great peace and this can manifest itself in the healer's eyes. Others will pick this up as a calm sensation. All healers will have a strong but calming energy around them which some people calls vibes. When a healer walks into a room a great feeling enters that space. The healer's guides or guide and the healer's energy bring this about.

At the end of this practice you will be buzzing and you will with practice be able to extend your energy field and project this energy to others in healing.

Now once again after standing there discharging energy, come back slowly out of the meditation, with the technique we used earlier and drink some water. Wash your hands or shake them towards the ground, but cut out any theatrical display, as it is best to keep things simple and natural. A lot of practitioners make a big issue out of this, and this can only be a distraction to themselves and to their clients. It makes a myth out of healing. Washing your hands is natural and has no myth, it is just good hygiene and as they say cleanliness is next to Godliness.

A simple experiment you can carry out on your friend or in a group for a bit of fun, to keep things light hearted and to help you progress. First draw both hands up in a circular fashion, palms facing outwards, circling your right hand in a clockwise direction and circle your left hand in an anti -clockwise direction, keeping

your hands in front of your chest about a face distance apart. Do this three times. This will unite the outer forces with the inner forces, the above and below the Alfa with the Omega and so bring balance and harmony within your space.

Next stand behind or in front of your friend and draw the imaginary figure eight three times, and fan out you hand with relaxed fingers as in the last practice. Now with the connection of both energies and the power of your mind move them forward or backwards as you're opposite energies (or auras meet). But your friend must relax totally and have full trust in you that you won't let them fall. This will help you both to let go and to gain confidence in each other. It will also help you both to gain confidence and trust in your abilities as a healer and to the esoteric nature of all things. This may seem like doing so called tricks, but just remember were allowed to have fun in life, as life is for living. We can use this exercise not alone for fun or to develop our healing potential, but we can heal others in this manner without perhaps them ever even knowing it. (Remember the thought is the deed.).

☯ Health Benefits of Releasing the circle

Opens up the Heart Chakra, Touch, Unconditional love, Forgiveness, Compassion, & Balance. It is associated with the thymus gland and controls the sense of touch, the heart, breasts, vaguest nerve, the blood circulation, the immune and endocrine system. It is also associated with peace, harmony, unconditional love and personal transformation. This Chakra vibrates to the colour of green, the colour of growth and transformation

When you have your own energy at a maximum level by tapping into the source you are able to discharge to others in healing or by helping them in some way. You are able to draw energy from the earth, as your feet will now act as huge conductors. You can do group healing, create energy fields, do absent or distance healing, teach others to heal and eventually heal the earth.

You can meditate and get the equivalent of two to three hours sleep. You can cut down on your intake of food. You can control your wants and desires so that they become optional. You will operate on a purer and spiritual level and reach your spiritual guide or higher -self.

Closure

A Final Word.

This book is purely inspirational and deals with healing in a truly open minded way. It was written mainly to take the myth out of healing and to stop it from been labelled and to acknowledge that healing has no boundaries.

This I hope will help people to be more open minded, so that healing is taken forward openly into the next millennium. We certainly need our doctors and scientists and the great work that they do. Indeed, some of them are natural healers but I think the time is fast approaching where doctors, scientists and healers will have to work together for the benefit of everyone on this planet. However, this is not to say that this planet may self-destruct or get hit by a comet. Man is in search of a new planet but it's a pity he can't take better care of this one and make it a safer place for the children of the future. This search will not solve all mans problems, not for a minute. Mans greed for power has always been his greatest pitfall and it drags him under into a dimension where he cannot find peace or rest. This mistake has been the misuse of power. Trying to hold on to this power is harmful in the Divine plan of things, as this power comes from the universal energy system and belongs to it. This is what all the great prophets of the past were telling us but sadly it was labelled and as one knows if we label something it must stay within boundaries. This is what has happened to our so-called religion of today. However, today, there is an ever-growing awareness of energy and of its therapeutic uses because of cosmic and interplanetary forces. This awareness can only be transformed into knowledge as we advance in psychic and science from the Piscean age to the Aquarian age, as uses of energy become a common occurrence in our homes and workplaces. This raising of awareness and use of energy will eventually lead to enlightenment for us all. Some could take a lifetime while others could take thousands of lifetimes, who knows? But we will all get there, thus changing a person's perception of the world around them. To give an example, when a person is in tune with their higher energy, they are also in tune with the higher vibrational rate of things and people around them. In short, they are in tune with the pleasant things in life; love, compassion, the colours of the trees and sky above them, the magnificence of a sunrise or sunset. When we are in harmony with the world around us then we have achieved the art of being. However, I believe that you will rapidly come to the conclusion that we are all moving and operating in the web of life, the web that has no weaver, and physics and science plays its part in this web. This is why today there are many people searching and from this search approaching the same point from many different directions. They will very shortly converge on that point and join hands and work together and this is the basic aim of this book and the function of the Castle. As I said, this all goes down to working with energy and vibrations. Even the vibrational rate of the planet itself is rising and there are those that will go with it and those that will not. It is true that there is much work to be done to make the transition as easy as possible and for as many people as possible and what would mankind do if it did not have its work. I honestly hope that in the future no one will label these writings and repeat the same mistake; will man ever learn? This mistake has been made throughout the centuries in religious cultures, beliefs and practices. One group of people thought that their culture or religion was better than the other. If he only realised that all of this is man made, for man, by man, for his quest for greed and power and not for his eternal glory. It will remain like this until man realises that there is no beginning or no end but that there is only the here and now and whatever he thinks, does or says lives with him forever. You are you forever and forever is the eternal here and now.

My spiritual guide finally says (inspirational wisdom). Man will only find true happiness and inner peace when he stops searching outside of himself through so called sensi, sifu or masters, spiritual directors, through various groups and organisations of one kind or another. He will only find happiness when he realises that he is his own master and that what he is searching for is already within.

The End.

Good luck with the practices in this book.

*If you want to find out more about my work,
and myself you can tap into a web site
www.trafford.com*

*They are doing my autobiography "The Journey Home", with outlets
in five countries Canada, UK, USA, Ireland and Spain.*

*If you have any questions or if you want to get in contact
with me, you can write to the address on the back of
the book. Take care and strive to be happy.*

About the Author

Charlie Shovlin lives Kilraine, Glenties, Co. Donegal, Ireland with his wife Grace.

Charles is one of the founding pioneers of Tai Chi in Ireland and is one of the first Irishmen to publishes a book on the subject. He has also produced and distributed his own Tai Chi DVD.

In 2006 he published his autobiography "The Journey Home".

He has taught and given many lectures and workshops on Tai Chi, Qigong and healing.

He is a renowned healer and people travel from all over Donegal and beyond to see him. He has appeared on RTE's Nationwide television programme in February 2002 and in 2016 he received a Master's in medical Qigong from the Renascent College, of Intuitive Science: Melbourne, Australia.

Other Works By Charles

Tai Chi For Everyone
ISBN 0-9545-7800-7

This book describes the postures, mainly taken for the Yang Cheng-Fu form of Taiji both moving and static with the help of photographs and diagrams and explains the health benefits that go with each posture. The author has made every effort to describe the exercises in as simple a way as possible. If you are a novice you should the DVD" Tai Chi for Everyone" a useful accompaniment to the book.

Order on line www.lulu.com

The Journey Home
ISBN 1-4120-6620-6

This book tells the story of the Castle and explained how the Castle Taiji Healing Centre was born. The Centre which allows him to see many clients on a regular basis, with the hope of bringing them some peace of mind, so that they too will find their niche- their own "Journey Home".

Order on line www.Trafford.com/05-513
Order on line www.Amazon.com
www.the-castle.8m.com
www.taichiworld.com

Lightning Source UK Ltd.
Milton Keynes UK
UKHW011138300821
389711UK00001B/114